VIRGINIA CITY
AND ALDER GULCH

KEN AND ELLEN SIEVERT

MONTANA MAGAZINE
AND
AMERICAN & WORLD GEOGRAPHIC PUBLISHING

THIS BOOK IS DEDICATED TO THE RESIDENTS OF VIRGINIA CITY: TO THOSE OF THE PAST WHO CREATED THE PLACE AND ITS HISTORY; TO THOSE WHO RECOGNIZED THE IMPORTANCE OF PRESERVING THAT HISTORY; AND TO THOSE OF THE PRESENT, WHO CONTINUE TO MAINTAIN ONE OF AMERICA'S TRULY SPECIAL PLACES.

WAYNE SCHERR

ACKNOWLEDGMENTS

At least as much history as gold appears to have poured out of Alder Gulch. We are indebted to all those who collected, recorded or preserved that history, as well as to those who helped assemble a veritable mountain of information for this slender volume. We are fortunate to have had the opportunity to write about Virginia City and would like to recognize those individuals who provided guidance to us during that effort. We are indebted to the Montana State Historic Preservation Office; curator John Ellingsen of Bovey Restorations; Jacqueline Pace for sharing the manuscripts written by Dick Pace; Ford and Sharon Bovey for generously sharing family history; Daryl Tichenor for the loan of files from the *Madisonian*; Ken and Sherri Deaver for their extensive research into the prehistory of the area; Bureau of Land Management in the Dillon Resource Area (particularly Bruce Botsford for shedding considerable light on the axolotl); Julianne Ruby, administrator of the archives at the Great Falls Public Library; and Richard Ecke at the *Great Falls Tribune*. Special thanks are in order to Dave Walter, research librarian at the Montana Historical Society, for his cheerful encouragement and skillful assistance.

Library of Congress
Cataloging-in-Publication Data

Sievert, Ken.
Virginia City and Alder Gulch / Ken and Ellen Sievert.
p. cm.
Includes bibliographical references and index.
ISBN 1-56037-041-6 :
1. Virginia City (Mont.)--History. 2. Virginia City (Mont.)--Guidebooks. 3. Alder (Mont.)--History. 4. Alder (Mont.)--Guidebooks. I. Sievert, Ellen. II. Title.
F739.V5S54 1993 93-19257
978.6'663--dc20

© 1993 American & World Geographic Publishing
Text © 1993 Ken & Ellen Sievert
All rights reserved.

This book may not be reproduced in whole or in part by any means (with the exception of short quotes for the purpose of review) without the permission of the publisher. For information, address American & World Geographic Publishing, P.O. Box 5630, Helena, MT 59604
Printed in Hong Kong

WAYNE SCHERR

CONTENTS

GEORGE WUERTHNER

Top: *Gold panning in twentieth-century Alder Gulch.*
Bottom: *Main Street of Nevada City, Montana.*

Facing page: *Along a Virginia City boardwalk.*
Title page: *Dry—but not boring—goods in Virginia City.* TOM DIETRICH

Front cover: *"The town stopped for a while to admire its own beauty."* TOM DIETRICH
Back cover, top: *The living past of Virginia City.* GARRY WUNDERWALD
Bottom: *Solitude in Nevada City.* DENNIS J. CWIDAK

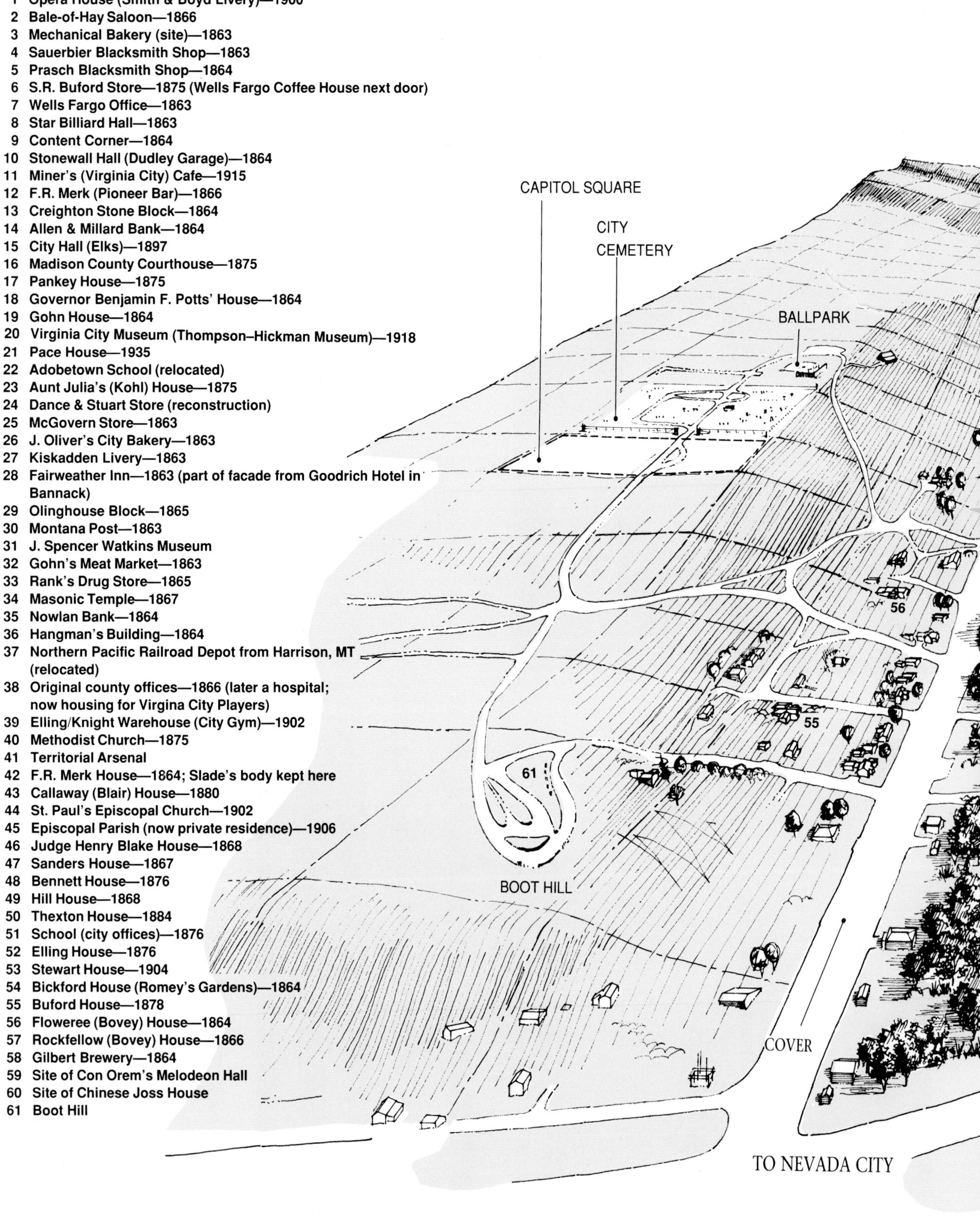

1 Opera House (Smith & Boyd Livery)—1900
2 Bale-of-Hay Saloon—1866
3 Mechanical Bakery (site)—1863
4 Sauerbier Blacksmith Shop—1863
5 Prasch Blacksmith Shop—1864
6 S.R. Buford Store—1875 (Wells Fargo Coffee House next door)
7 Wells Fargo Office—1863
8 Star Billiard Hall—1863
9 Content Corner—1864
10 Stonewall Hall (Dudley Garage)—1864
11 Miner's (Virginia City) Cafe—1915
12 F.R. Merk (Pioneer Bar)—1866
13 Creighton Stone Block—1864
14 Allen & Millard Bank—1864
15 City Hall (Elks)—1897
16 Madison County Courthouse—1875
17 Pankey House—1875
18 Governor Benjamin F. Potts' House—1864
19 Gohn House—1864
20 Virginia City Museum (Thompson–Hickman Museum)—1918
21 Pace House—1935
22 Adobetown School (relocated)
23 Aunt Julia's (Kohl) House—1875
24 Dance & Stuart Store (reconstruction)
25 McGovern Store—1863
26 J. Oliver's City Bakery—1863
27 Kiskadden Livery—1863
28 Fairweather Inn—1863 (part of facade from Goodrich Hotel in Bannack)
29 Olinghouse Block—1865
30 Montana Post—1863
31 J. Spencer Watkins Museum
32 Gohn's Meat Market—1863
33 Rank's Drug Store—1865
34 Masonic Temple—1867
35 Nowlan Bank—1864
36 Hangman's Building—1864
37 Northern Pacific Railroad Depot from Harrison, MT (relocated)
38 Original county offices—1866 (later a hospital; now housing for Virgina City Players)
39 Elling/Knight Warehouse (City Gym)—1902
40 Methodist Church—1875
41 Territorial Arsenal
42 F.R. Merk House—1864; Slade's body kept here
43 Callaway (Blair) House—1880
44 St. Paul's Episcopal Church—1902
45 Episcopal Parish (now private residence)—1906
46 Judge Henry Blake House—1868
47 Sanders House—1867
48 Bennett House—1876
49 Hill House—1868
50 Thexton House—1884
51 School (city offices)—1876
52 Elling House—1876
53 Stewart House—1904
54 Bickford House (Romey's Gardens)—1864
55 Buford House—1878
56 Floweree (Bovey) House—1864
57 Rockfellow (Bovey) House—1866
58 Gilbert Brewery—1864
59 Site of Con Orem's Melodeon Hall
60 Site of Chinese Joss House
61 Boot Hill
CAPITOL SQUARE
CITY CEMETERY
BALLPARK
56
55
61
BOOT HILL
COVER
TO NEVADA CITY

The Town of Virginia City 1993

VISITORS PLEASE NOTE: *Many of the houses identified on this drawing are privately owned. Please respect the privacy of the residents.*

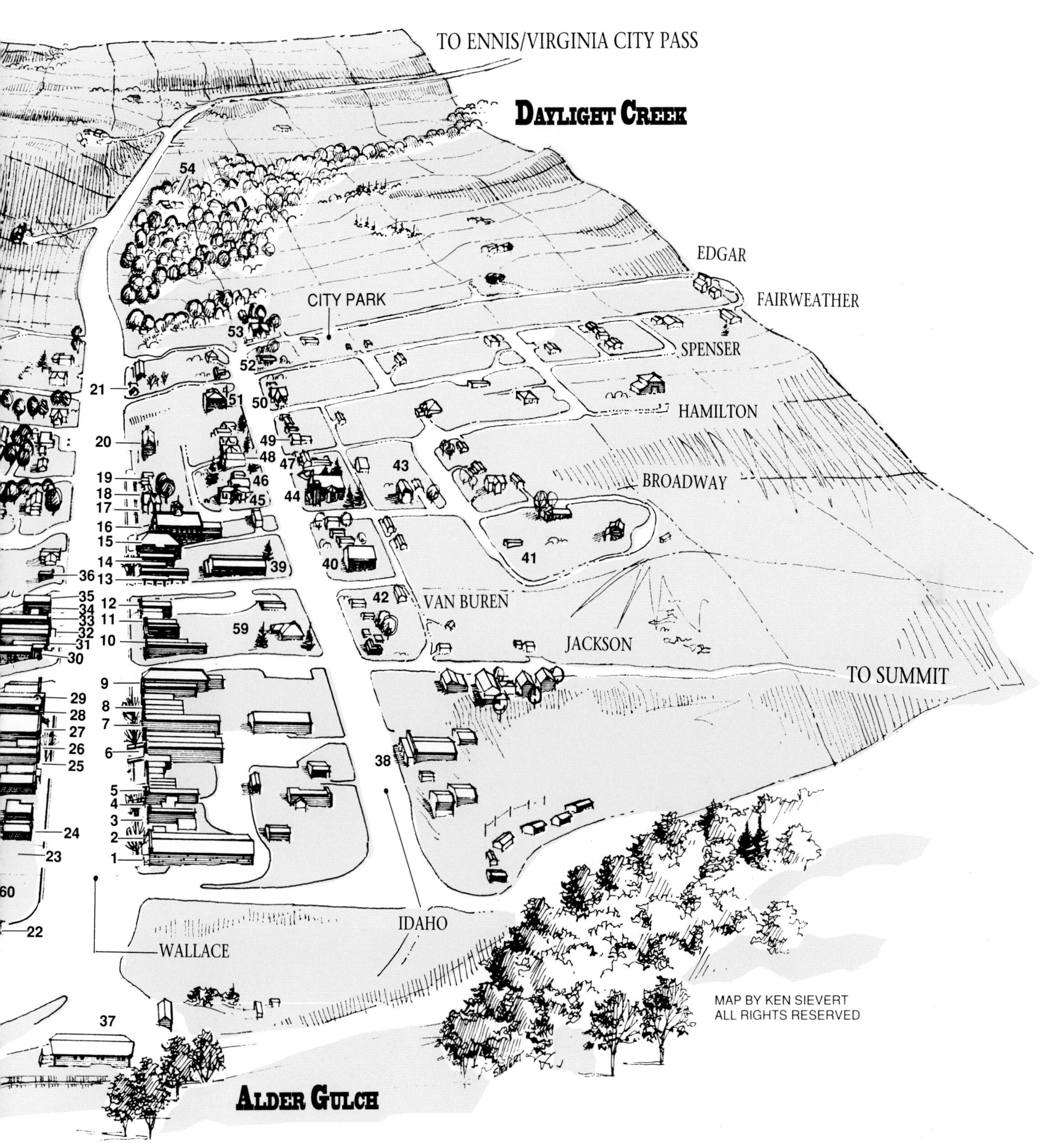

GARRY WUNDERWALD PHOTOS

Right: *A day in Nevada City when a miner might have been frozen out of his "digs."*
Below: *"Remoteness makes us what we are," offered one Virginia City resident.*

DENNIS J. CWIDAK

The hush of the off-season in Nevada City.

THE CLIMATE

There is a word for Montana's weather—unpredictable. Residents have all shoveled "ten percent chance of precipitation" from walks and drives, and enjoyed the adage: "If you don't like the weather, wait five minutes and it will change." The weather's capricious reputation is certainly earned in Alder Gulch.

Nestled in a small "pocket" of the mountains, at an elevation of around 5,800 feet, Virginia City has a micro-climate all its own. Expect warm, sunny, blue sky days and cool nights in the summer. The same brilliant sunshine, blue sky (and blue ski-wax) days occur in the winter, when the hush of snowfall equals the hush of the "off-season" community. The sunshine and the light, dry air is said to result in an "expansive physical feeling and a heartier and more cordial spirit," noted James Handly in his 1872 report on *The Resources of Madison County*.

Seasons and climate add an interesting dimension to the natural and man-made resources of Virginia City and Alder Gulch, and their extremes accentuate historical stories. Temperatures here range from a normal minimum of 10.6 degrees Fahrenheit on a January day to a normal maximum of 81.3 degrees on a July day. The coldest month on record was January 1875, with an average temperature of 1.7 degrees. July 1916 had the warmest average, 73.5 degrees. The record low at the nearest weather station, in Dillon, was 36 degrees below zero in 1937; the record high was 101 degrees, in 1961.

Winter is a fine time to visit Virginia City, keeping in mind that one restaurant, one bar, maybe one bed and breakfast, and one general store have to serve all your needs. Since residents of Virginia City must travel to outlying communities for access to schools, medical attention, and supplies, Highway 287 is kept well plowed.

Without the lines of cars, recreational vehicles, and tourists, the winter magic of Virginia City comes alive. One can easily imagine the difficulties experienced by residents in 1865, when a great share of the "importations" were brought overland a distance of more than 2,500 miles. Teams and wagons battled the snow-clogged trails to their destination with no carefully plowed highways to ease their passage.

Visualize a Virginia City merchant in the winter of 1864-65, viewing his emptying shelves with no hope of fresh supplies. That was the year teams couldn't get through and the price of flour rocketed to one dollar per pound from about 27¢. Walk down Wallace Street in mid-winter and imagine the nearly 500 men who marched into the community and, under the banner of an empty flour sack, demanded flour at a fair price.

The thaws of May did bring sixty-four sacks of flour into the community and the price dropped to $65 per bag, about 66¢ per pound. Nathaniel P. Langford described the changing seasons in *Vigilante Days and Ways:*

> The snow crust was melting, and oxen and mules sank out of sight. The flour that did arrive had been unloaded three times and carried 200 yards at a stretch on the shoulders of straining, floundering men. Another 107 sacks came in, but the mules carrying the mail had not got through.

Don your snowshoes or skis (snowmobiles, if you must, but they tend to disturb ghosts) and glide through the Gulch area. Imagine the party that arrived in January of 1866 and reported snow piled up 25 to 30 feet between Dry Creek and the Junction. They had traveled a distance of only five miles in one day's time.

The popularity of hurdy-gurdies (dance halls/saloons) and other delights, for miners frozen out of their "digs" is also readily understood if Virginia City is visited in winter.

There is a building on Wallace Street well known as the Hangman's Building. Showing its age after 129 years of use and exposure to the

DENNIS J. CWIDAK

As an unfinished structure, the Hangman's Building in Virginia City provided the beam from which Vigilantes hanged five criminals in the cold winter of 1864.

elements, it served the community for many years as a drugstore. Stand in front of it on a January day and recall the winter of 1864, when the then unfinished building provided the beam on which Vigilantes hanged five road agents and murderers.

The changing seasons are inclined to be a little awkward at times, and slipping into the fall of 1865, the *Montana Post* reported on an October day:

> We, in this part of the moral vineyard have not been able to sing "everything is lovely and the goose hangs high" during the past week. The rain has come down, with but little intermission, making mud roofs hideous, and the geese above referred to have uttered the notes of preparation for a journey to more sunny climes.

View the quaint dwellings along the Gulch and consider how living with a dirt floor below and a sod roof above could indeed be hideous in times of rain.

Fortunately, the average annual precipitation is a mere 16.26 inches, more than that of the valley floors nearby, but less than falls on the adjacent mountain tops. Weather records from Virginia City suggest that approximately 60 percent of this is in the form of snow. Average annual snowfall is 38.8 inches. Soaking rains are uncommon in summer and fall. Residents don't generally own or use umbrellas, as is the case with many Montana natives.

The miners ravished the Gulch over the years, denuding it of the flora, removing trees and shrubs both for access to the earth and to provide materials for crude shelters. Opening and reopening the "vaults" of Alder Gulch left the landscape a picture of waste and destruction. With the vaults emptied (maybe...), nature has continued the task of softening the land with vegetation.

Most folks prefer to visit Virginia City during the summer season, when the Virginia City Players entertain in the Opera House and vaudeville shows are in full swing in the Brewery. Bed and breakfasts, restaurants and bars triple in number, and the Fairweather Inn and Nevada City Hotel offer lodging. A variety of shops open and exhibits relating to mining-camp life offer visitors insight into the 1860s.

Heat and hustle join to elicit images of the days when nearly 10,000 people resided in the Gulch, and Independence Day provided a joyous cause for celebration in Virginia City. In *Golden Gulch*, Dick Pace describes Fourth of July celebrations that took place until after World War I:

> Speeches, banquets and contests were popular but the highlight of the day was the firing of the cannon into Cannon-ball Hill across Daylight Gulch from the courthouse. Everyone enjoyed this; everyone that is but Abe Martin, whose cabin was too close to the target for comfort.

Rock-drilling contests drew huge crowds, as did the pair of miners who amazed Fourth of July crowds, for several years, by "walking a tightrope between the courthouse and the City Hall."

With a climate "better than some places, worse than others," Larry Barsness concluded in *Gold Camp* (1962), "The natural beauty of the surrounding country must have moved all but the most molelike miner." He had more to say:

> Sunsets here beat anything a man ever saw back home, some nights filling the whole sky with color. And the special sunset that came sometimes after a rain, when the sun dropped into a slit between purple clouds and skyline, gilding rough lumber buildings with colored light, redoing the dull hillside in bold-lighted rock and juniper against purple-shadowed gullies...The town stopped for a while to admire its own beauty.

JOHN REDDY

KENT & CHARLENE KRONE

__Above:__ Bell Lake north of Virginia City in the Tobacco Root Mountains, which are steep and alpine.
__Top:__ Gravelly Range to the south is not as heavily timbered and exhibits vegetation more closely related to mountain steppe environments.

THE LAND

Virginia City was built near the mouth of Daylight Creek, which drains the west side of the low saddle that connects the Tobacco Root Mountains to the Gravelly Range into Alder Gulch. The town is surrounded by a rich mixture of landforms, plant types, wildlife, and geologic upheavals that characterize southwestern Montana. It is located in that corner of the state that builds up to the elevated and still-active cauldron of Yellowstone National Park; it is also part of the wrinkled landscape that ultimately sorts itself out into the headwaters of the Missouri River. Not far to the west is the Continental Divide, the weathermaking backbone of the Rockies that separates Montana's upland valleys and mountains from the Great Basin and the Columbia River country.

Like two giant furrows in the landscape, the Madison and Jefferson valleys parallel one another for over seventy-five miles—separated only by the spine of the Gravelly and Tobacco Root mountains—until they finally come together with the Gallatin River at the Three Forks of the Missouri. The valley floors of the major drainages have been leveled by time and are pastoral; the intervening mountains are magnificently sculpted. The upper end of the Jefferson Valley collects the waters of the Big Hole, Beaverhead, and Ruby rivers. Waters draining Alder Gulch flow into the Ruby.

James Handly's 1872 description of the mountains was less than scientific:

> Naturalists and Geologists will find in whichever direction they turn attention, the book of nature wide open with problems, inviting their most earnest study, inscribed upon its pages...At all times and seasons there is something grand, majestical and attractive in [the mountains'] appearance. Whether in the morning, when they are first illuminated by the rays of the rising sun, and the mist in tall vapory columns ascends to the skies as incense; at mid-day, when the rough, rugged, broken sides ornamented with evergreens catch in turn the ever-varying reflections of sunlight and shade; in the evening, when the last departing rays of sunlight rests for a moment on their brow ere vanishing from the horizon; at night, when the massive and towering rocks assume the appearance of ancient castles and fortresses, their domes and turrets receiving the light of the shining concave...

According to Handly, the most scenic mountain range in Montana is the Ruby Range, across the Ruby Valley immediately west of Virginia City. The Rubies are highly visible from the town and during sunsets they are the front curtain of a stage-set that includes the Pioneer and Highland ranges as backdrops farther northwest. Although not visible from Virginia City, the upper Ruby River carves yet another mountain range off of the elevated plateau of the Gravelly Range—

GEORGE WUERTHNER

DIANE ENSIGN

Above: *Pastoral scene along the Ruby River nearing Virginia City.* ***Top:*** *Baldy Mountain in the Gravelly Range.* ***Right:*** *Ruby River Reservoir, south of Alder.*

PHIL FARNES

the majestic Snowcrests, which display nearly perpetual snow. Numerous other ranges in the vicinity delight those with a proclivity for the prodigious pointy landforms: the Elkhorn Range is to the west; the Centennials cross the southern end of Madison County; and the Taylor–Hilgard Mountains extend along the eastern border, culminating in the pristine Spanish Peaks Wilderness Area.

Although joined at the ends and of similar elevation, the Tobacco Root Mountains and the Gravelly Range are considerably different in character. The Gravellys are more rolling and rounded, less heavily timbered, and exhibit vegetative growth more closely related to mountain "steppe" environments; the Tobacco Roots are steep, incised, and alpine. Wildflowers are profuse in both ranges throughout the short growing season, although the varieties differ.

From a distant view, it is apparent that the Madison Valley and a part of the Jefferson Valley were once inland seas. The ancient shorelines can still be seen along the flanks of the ranges.

Some 400 million years ago, the foundations for the landforms at Virginia City were laid by heat-altered and pressured granites; and as the land rose, fell, crumpled, and shrank, the mountains emerged. Many millions of years later, massive volcanic flows of basalt spilled across the ridges east of the town to give yet another dimension to the puzzling rock formations encountered by the miners. A few tertiary lake beds added geologic garnish to the recipe that localized the rare shining metal—gold.

The stream of Alder Gulch has done its carving throughout the centuries and was described by the Virginia City Mining Company as "The Greatest Natural Sluice in America."

THE FIRST ONES

Because of its proximity to the Continental Divide, the southwest corner of what became Montana Territory was influenced by plains, plateau, and coastal cultures, making a prehistoric "melting pot."

The site is relatively close to the immigration route of ancient peoples that started at the Bering land bridge and continued southward into the Americas. Imagination suggests that some of those following the trail diffused into the Madison, Jefferson, and Beaverhead valleys, or roamed into the headwater lands of the Columbia River, or even camped along Alder Gulch. Ethnologists, archaeologists, anthropologists, and specialists on the historic environment continue to probe into the human occupation of the area over the millennia. Madison County is particularly rich in prehistoric evidence of occupation. There is carbon-dated evidence of occupation 8,800 years old within the region. Researchers sponsored by the Bureau of Land Management (BLM) so far have surveyed over fifty prehistoric sites within the county on BLM land alone.

Interpretation of the evidence to date suggests that the area has been continuously inhabited by a wide diversity of cultures affected over time by planetary temperature and moisture swings, cultural growth and exchange, and changes resulting from external pressures and increased mobility. The area seems to have been a place of stability and refuge during times when conditions were unfavorable in adjacent, more exposed environments. With the range of altitudes and seasons providing a variety of edible plants for man and animal, and geologic formations providing the quarries for tools and implements, the residents of prehistory occupied the place leaving us hints of their existence; and much to ponder.

Culturally and geographically, Virginia City is part of the headwaters of the Missouri River, near the headwaters of the Columbia River, and is easily reached from the great southwest basin west of the Rockies. It lies forty to fifty miles northeast of the Great Bannock Trail that ancient hunters crossed seasonally between the headwaters of the Snake and Yellowstone rivers.

JOHN REDDY

The Fort Laramie Treaty of 1868 ending the Indian wars closed the Bozeman Trail to white travelers.

The use of the Virginia City area by numerous groups of Indian people at the time of white infiltration is underscored when the historic records from 1800 to 1890 are reviewed. In 1805, Lewis and Clark encountered Sacagawea's people, the Shoshone, at nearby Beaverhead Rock (Point-of-Rocks). Three years later, one of the expedition's former sergeants, John Colter, was captured by the Blackfeet while trapping downstream at Three Forks. The Flathead people visited Bannack (founded in 1862), as did the Bannocks and Sheep-Eaters. The Cree camped at the outskirts of Virginia City after the town was founded.

Cultural conflict was the norm at the time gold was discovered in Alder Gulch, and it was to have an impact on the camp. Travel to Virginia City along the Bozeman and Bridger trails was slowed and eventually stopped altogether as a condition of the treaty that ended the 1864-68 Indian wars. There were "forts" in the area but they were not military posts, but trading posts. Citizen militias were created according to need, or in some cases, according to perceived need. James Fergus, associated with the Fairweather Mining District in 1863, and later a Madison County Commissioner, summed up the conditions in the early 1860s:

> There is no doubt but the Indians have

Looking south from the cemetery to Virginia City, circa 1920.

murdered and plundered a great many whites. But so far as my experience goes during the past winter the whites have been the aggressors and the Indians have behaved theirselves by far the most civilized people. Many of the rowdies here think it fine fun to shoot an Indian.

Fort Ellis, which was constructed in the Gallatin Valley in 1867, had a stabilizing influence on the population.

Although Virginia City was not directly affected by the 1877 flight and fight of Chief Joseph and the Nez Percé in their historic bid for freedom, the town did mobilize a militia to support the regular Army in pursuit of Joseph, and it also served as a source of supplies for the troops. Colonel James E. Callaway of Virginia City raised a company of volunteers, and on August 19 they rode fifty miles south to join General Howard at Camas Meadows. That night the Nez Percé backtracked and ran off the army's mules as well as all but one of the volunteers' horses; the militia returned home afoot.

In the winter of 1877-78, poor conditions on the Bannock Indian reservation prompted raids on the settlers in the upper Ruby Valley by the Bannock and Nez Percé, causing some concern for the residents of Virginia City. The settlers garrisoned at Puller Springs in the upper Ruby Valley; there was no fighting or property damage although area ranchers lost considerable stock.

The reduced lifestyles of the Indian people in the Virginia City area is poignantly told in the story of "Mattie," as recounted in Wylie Davis's oral history, which is archived at the Bozeman High School Library. Mattie was an older Bannock woman who lived in her lodge (tipi) above Virginia City in the late 1800s when Davis was growing up there. She did housework and other chores for local residents for her minimal subsistence for many years; she also provided diversion and some education for small boys of the town who probably had little opportunity to interface with other cultures and customs.

MONTANA HISTORICAL SOCIETY PHOTOS BOTH PAGES

***Above:** Virginia City in the mid-1860s, an era which saw the arrival of telegraph service, public schools, and churches.*
***Left:** McGovern's Store in Virginia City, about 1930. Mary McGovern (pictured) is reputed to have placed an* Out to Lunch *sign on the door as a means of declaring retirement. Charles Bovey bought it all, lock, dry goods, and barrel.*

Henry Edgar in August 1899. Edgar was one of the six prospectors who panned the gravels of Alder Creek on May 26, 1863, precipitating the gold rush to the Gulch.

The Discovery

Although there are scattered reports that predate 1860 regarding the discovery of gold in the territory that was to become Montana, the first substantive discovery that resulted in a permanent mining settlement occurred at Bannack.

It was, however, the discovery of gold along Alder Gulch, in combination with westward migration patterns and improved transportation routes that lit the fuse for an explosion of growth, activity, politics, vigilantism, and cultural transposition that was equaled at few other places in the west. The instant city that emerged from the gold-laden gravels of Alder Gulch was Virginia City. The year was 1863.

Prospectors Thomas Cover, Henry Edgar, Bill Fairweather, Barney Hughes, Harry Rodgers, and Michael Sweeney arrived at the gulch in the late afternoon of May 26, 1863, on their way home to Bannack. They were returning from a gold-seeking expedition to the Yellowstone Valley, where they had been captured and held by the Crow people. They had negotiated their freedom by bartering their horses and by convincing their captors that they had power in the spirit world—Bill Fairweather, having no fear of snakes, put a large rattlesnake inside his shirt. The Crow immediately released the gold-seekers.

During the early evening of the 26th, in the habit of prospectors, they panned the gravels of Alder Creek. First Fairweather, then Edgar saw "colors" (traces of gold), and by nightfall the six had recovered enough of the rare metal to realize that this was an important discovery. When they returned to Bannack to replace their confiscated supplies, their freshly filled pokes caught the attention of other miners. It proved impossible for the party to return to their new discovery without a large band of followers. After striking an agreement that they would be allowed to stake the first claims, the discoverers led their entourage of some 200 miners to Alder Gulch.

Developments at the Gulch took place at a rapid-fire pace, and then gained momentum. Mining began in earnest, with little thought given to shelter or supplies. Some miners just slept under the stars during that summer of 1863. Some used brush wickiups, tents, shallow caves, or trees for shelter. They were far too intent on collecting the bounty of the earth to waste time building homes or planning for the needs of the upcoming winter season.

There were some "old-timers," but for the most part, the miners were relatively young men, out to make their fortunes and return home, some to families left behind.

Gold comes in many forms, however, and not all of the influx was devoted to mining. Enterprising developers and merchants also responded to the news of the strike. After making sure the land was devoid of gold, a company quickly formed to claim 320 acres for a townsite. On June 16, 1863, Virginia City was born, incorporated by a miners' court.

Among developers, competition for establishing townsites was keen, as being on the ground floor of nearly any enterprise boosted chances of success. With an exploding population in the Gulch, Nevada City entrepreneurs vied with those in Virginia City to develop a substantial service community. The other five cities of the Gulch—Junction City, Adobetown, Central City, Union City (for the Northerners in this third year of the Civil War), and Summit—followed suit.

Before a year had elapsed, the Alder Gulch area had an estimated population of 7,000 or more, housed mainly in crude, sod-roofed log cabins or impromptu shelters. The mining districts of Granite, Brown's Gulch, Highland, and Pine Grove filled in the gaps between, or next to the towns.

The first permanent commercial building in Virginia City, the Mechanical Bakery, was built in 1863. A.J. Oliver established stage service to the town that first year as well, and pony express service was established to Fort Bridger, Utah. The first church service was held in the fall, and the first hanging by vigilantes occurred December 21, 1863.

VIGILANTES AND INNOCENTS

The growth may have been too fast, the society disorganized, the wealth too great, or the "law" too unstructured; for whatever reasons, Virginia City, its sister city of Bannack, and the traveled routes to the states became the scenes of robberies and murders by a cunningly organized band of the lawless. Insight into the conditions prevalent at the new "diggin's" is found in the *Reminiscences of Alexander Toponce:*

> The discovery of Alder Gulch attracted the greatest aggregation of toughs and criminals that ever got together in the west. They came up the Missouri River on the steamboats by the scores, deserters from the Union and Rebel armies, river pirates and professional gamblers and sharpers.
>
> They came by wagon trains from the gold camps of Nevada and California and by pack trains across the divide from the Columbia River country and they came in from Pike's Peak camps, to which adventurers had flocked from all over the east.

Recognizing the towns' vulnerability, the lawless quickly developed an organization, led by Henry Plummer. He arrived in Bannack in 1862, with a history of violence and crime, and a network of contacts with former prisonmates and toughs of similar ilk. Plummer organized this collection effectively and efficiently. Calling themselves the Innocents, they helped elect Plummer sheriff of Bannack in May of 1863. With the Rattlesnake Ranch near Bannack as their headquarters, the outlaws infiltrated and controlled some businesses as well as the gold camp transportation routes. Encouraged by the lack of resistance, the Innocents became bolder, more violent, and committed their crimes more frequently and with less provocation. It is estimated that the gang was responsible for 102 murders and the thievery of $250,000 worth of gold.

But resistance did organize—in the form of vigilantes. Outraged by the murders of George Evans, D.H. Dillingham, and some friendly

JOHN REDDY

Robbers' Roost, downstream from Alder Gulch. This stagecoach stop was reputed to be one of the meeting places of the Plummer gang.

MONTANA HISTORICAL SOCIETY

The Hangman's Building on Wallace Street in Virginia City served the community for many years as a drugstore.

Bannock Indians, the Vigilantes decided that they had to act when young Nicholas Tiebalt (variously spelled *Tbalt* and *Thiebalt*) was murdered over a span of mules. The citizens tracked down the killer, road agent George Ives, tried him in open miners' court, and hanged him in Nevada City on December 21, 1863. During the next forty-four days the "stranglers" systematically dispensed frontier justice. To notify suspects, the Vigilantes used the mysterious symbol 3-7-77. The most widely held belief, although not the most plausible, is that it signified grave dimensions—3 feet wide, 7 feet long, and 77 inches deep. The Vigilantes hanged twenty-three of the road agents, including the outlaw Sheriff Plummer, publicly flogged others, and banished many more from their camps.

One particular evening, January 13, 1864, found Virginia City encircled by more than 500 armed men, while the Vigilante Executive Committee pondered the evidence of guilt against road agents, thieves, and murderers. The "cordon of iron men was quietly stretching along the height overlooking the city" ready to prevent the escape of those found guilty by the committee. In *Vigilante Days and Ways,* Nathaniel P. Langford, described the day:

> Morning broke, cold and cloudy, discovering to the eyes of the citizens the pickets of the Vigilantes. The city was like an entrenched camp. Hundreds of men, with guns at the shoulder, were marching through the snow on all the surrounding hillsides, with military regularity and precision. The preparation could not have been more perfect if made to oppose an invading army. There was no misunderstanding this array. People talked with bated breath to each other of the certain doom which awaited the villains who had so long preyed upon their substance, and spread terror through the country.

In the brisk winter morning of January 14, 1864, the armed Vigilantes and hundreds of spectators lined the two streets adjacent to a building with an exposed beam. Boone Helm, Jack Gallagher, Frank Parrish, Hayes Lyons, and George Lane, duly tried and convicted, answered to the Vigilantes acting upon Wilbur Fisk Sanders' command, "Men, do your duty."

The self-imposed law and order of the Vigilantes has long been debated, viewed as a necessity by some, and with horror by others. The citizens in the isolated region needed protection and were ready for the laws of the courts to replace the laws of the Vigilantes.

WAYNE SCHERR

MONTANA HISTORICAL SOCIETY

THE ROUTES

Montana was one of the last places in the west to be infiltrated by the advancing tide of white Americans. Although the area was crisscrossed by early explorers, trappers, hunters, surveyors, and nomadic adventurers, permanent European-influenced settlement barely existed outside of Fort Benton and the Bitterroot Valley until the discovery of gold in Bannack and Virginia City. First a rivulet and then a flood, when the in-migration began, it occurred primarily along three distinct routes.

Disappointed fortune seekers from California and Colorado came north through Utah into Idaho Territory, along what came to be known as the Montana Trail. From the east, emigrants followed the Oregon Trail as far as Deer Creek Crossing (Glenrock) and Red Buttes (Casper, Wyoming) to head north on the Bozeman Trail or the Bridger Trail, or continued on to Salt Lake City and Fort Hall to join the Montana Trail if they were troubled by reports of prairie warfare on the shorter routes. The third route was by way of steamboat up the Missouri River to Fort Benton, and then along the newly completed Mullan Road before turning south to the gold camps. Although used to a lesser degree, a fourth route of commerce from Washington Territory either followed the Oregon Trail back to Salt Lake City and then headed north, or else followed the Mullan Road east to Hellgate and Deer Lodge to enter the area.

Steamboat navigation to Fort Benton started in 1860 with the arrival of the *Chippewa*, and river traffic was considerable until after the Civil War, when the overland routes became more traveled. River travel on the upper Missouri relied on sufficient inflow and was seasonal at best.

The Montana Trail left the Oregon Trail at Corinne, Utah, and ran through Fort Hall, Idaho, en route to southwestern Montana. It was consistently and continuously used, first by pioneers like the Stuart brothers, to avoid the "Mormon Wars" in Utah Territory, and later by many others when the conflicts in Utah ended and emigrants flooded across the Great American Desert. It proved to be the safest overland route during the 1864-1868 Indian wars, but it was the longest overland route from the states, and perhaps the least safe from road agents prior to Vigilante justice.

Two "cut-off" roads crossed Wyoming with shorter routes. The road scouted by Jim Bridger across central Wyoming was the shortest, but it had stretches of bad water and poor grass. Five wagon trains followed this route in 1864, but it was not used after that.

The Bozeman Trail northward through eastern Wyoming—mapped by John Bozeman and John Jacobs—encroached on hunting reserves of the Sioux and Cheyenne. The first wagon train of 1863 was turned back at Powder River by the Indians, who were becoming

***Above:** The town of Ruby was built in 1901 to accommodate employees of the dredging companies in the Gulch, which were active from 1897 through 1922.*
***Top:** Nevada City. Coaches were originally for mail and gradually evolved to offer comfort to passengers.*

TOM DIETRICH

***Above:** Nevada City was a bustling part of the Alder Gulch "14-mile city" complex of the 1860s, with a population of several hundred. Dredging operations destroyed much of the evidence of the community.*

***Facing page:** The Buford Store in the historic district of Virginia City.*

increasingly alarmed by the numbers of emigrants they saw crossing the prairie. Several wagon trains followed the trail in 1864, however, and more came in 1865. In 1866 the army built three posts along the Bozeman Trail—Fort Phil Kearny, Fort C.F. Smith, and Fort Reno (originally Fort Conner). Ironically, the forts caused an increase in hostilities and the route became more dangerous after the posts were manned. On November 6, 1868, a new treaty was signed with Red Cloud, Oglala Sioux leader, and its provision that the forts be vacated marked the end of use of the Bozeman Trail.

A northern overland route from Minnesota was pioneered by Captain James Fisk, but was seldom used, and the Sawyer Trail from Niobrara City, Dakota, was used only once as an alternative to the Oregon Trail.

Mail and news between the territories and the states was always a concern. The limited pony express that connected Bannack and Fort Bridger, Utah in 1863 soon gave way to stagecoaches that were for mail first and passengers second. Coaches were rough, drafty, and too hot or too cold depending on the season. They were manned by a breed that was generally capable but often less than gentle.

A.J. Oliver and Conover established the first stage route between Virginia City and Salt Lake in 1863, followed by the well-known western coachman Ben Holladay, who started a rival line in 1864 and quickly eliminated the competition by lowering fares. Holladay remained the king of the stage business until 1866 when he sold to Overland–Wells Fargo. The stage business adapted and gradually improved for passengers. The major lines served the longer routes and contracted to carry mail, while smaller independents provided service between the numerous towns and camps springing up in the gulches and coulees.

As the dashing stages and their colorful drivers carried mail and passengers, the goods, tools, foodstuffs, and machinery labored along the trails at the hands of the freighters. Freight to Virginia City and other camps originated at Fort Benton, Corinne, or Walla Walla, with a smaller amount from the distant east arriving along the Bozeman Trail. Plodding muscular oxen furnished most of the power for this massive work, although multiple spans of mules were preferred by some. The mule skinners and bull whackers moved from six to seven million pounds of goods annually—at an average cost of about ten cents per pound—from the stockpile at Corinne.

It is estimated that 600 freighters were engaged in the Montana trade in 1873, including independents, farmers who needed extra income, and major broad-based freight outfits such as Kirkendall Consolidated, Far West Freight, and the Diamond R.

Railroads eventually replaced most of the major stage and freight routes. The narrow gauge Utah and Northern reached Dillon on October 5, 1880, and Butte the following year. The Northern Pacific crossed the Territory from east to west, completing the work in 1883. Stages continued to provide transportation as "feeders" for the railroad by serving the more remote communities. Some of the stage routes lasted until nearly 1920.

GEORGE WUERTHNER

JOHN REDDY

The Acting One, Thomas Francis Meagher, in front of the state capitol in Helena. In the early 1900s when wealthy Irish of Butte funded the sculpture, this was the "backyard" of the capitol.

Montana Territory

The work of Sidney Edgerton did not go unnoticed by the Lincoln administration. Edgerton, who served in Congress during the trying times which preceded the Civil War, had been a member of the group which formed the Republican Party in 1856. He was first elected to Congress in 1858, and at the completion of two terms as Representative from Ohio, he was appointed Chief Justice of the newly formed Territory of Idaho, of which Virginia City and Bannack were a part. He likely believed that his duties in the "wilderness" would take him far away from problems associated with a nation at war with itself.

Edgerton and his nephew, Wilbur F. Sanders, and their families left Akron in June of 1863. From Missouri, the group went up river to Omaha, where they "outfitted, and then essayed to annihilate distance...with ox-teams as the motive power."

The party arrived in Bannack, Idaho Territory, on September 17, 1863, and the "worn out oxen were unyoked on Yankee Flats." Winter was imminent and the bulk of the mining population from his assigned post in Bannack had already flocked to Alder Gulch, answering the call of another big strike.

Sidney Edgerton soon realized that Idaho Territory was a geographic impossibility. Hundreds of miles, severe weather, and the massive Rocky Mountains separated the eastern district from the territorial capital at Lewiston. Only mining-camp law "governed" the communities so far removed from the center of government.

At the urging of Con Orem, well-known mining camp pugilist and street-corner orator, Edgerton and Wilbur F. Sanders quickly joined others in the crusade to divide Idaho Territory. Because of his connections in Washington, D.C. and his political acumen, Edgerton was selected to make the trip to Washington to plead the case for division of the territory. Citizens eager for more effective government took up a collection of cash to finance the trip, and a collection of gold for "show."

His traveling party waited until after the Vigilantes had "done their duty" on January 14, thus removing one major obstacle to travel. Writer Tom Stout said that Edgerton planned to carry "immense nuggets wherewith to dazzle the eyes of congressmen and to impress on their minds by means of an object lesson some adequate idea of the great mineral wealth of this section of the country."

The party left January 24, 1864, traveling with pack horses to Salt Lake, into the bitter winter weather. The hardships decreased at Salt Lake, where a stage was available to take them east to the railroad.

In Washington, Representative James M. Ashley of Ohio, chairman of the U.S. Committee on Territories, had already laid the groundwork for the creation of a new territory, including the selection of the name Montana.

Congressmen were easily dazzled by the borrowed gold, since they needed to replenish the Civil War coffers and a wealthy new territory would mean additional taxes. Ashley's bill to create a temporary government for Montana Territory met little opposition. The bill easily passed both Senate and House, and on Wednesday, May 26, President Abraham Lincoln affixed his signature, and the Territory of Montana became a reality.

The 1864 Organic Act drafted by Congress served as a framework to create a government for the new territory. It defined boundaries that have remained unchanged, except for correction of minor technical errors. Basic guidelines for establishment and operation of executive, legislative, and judicial branches were also included in the document and, as was the case with most western territories, it allowed the president to appoint the executive and judicial officers. Citizens were given the right to elect seven Territorial Council members and thirteen Assembly members, as well as one representative to Congress, who was allowed a "voice," but not a vote.

Sidney Edgerton was appointed governor of Montana Territory. Nathaniel P. Langford was appointed Collector of Internal Revenue, but the position of Territorial Secretary remained unfilled.

Without a secretary, whose most important function was to disburse federal funds, Edgerton used his own or borrowed funds to begin the task of creating a government for the fledgling territory. Politicians back in the States had their hands full with a raging civil war, and issues in far-away places like Montana Territory were not high priority in Washington. The appointment of a Territorial Secretary for Montana was not made until after the war ended and a new administration was in place following the assassination of Lincoln in April of 1865.

Edgerton had a hasty census taken in order to lay out the districts for the election of the Council and Assembly positions called for in the Organic Act. He learned that of the 15,822 residents in the whole territory, 11,493 resided in Madison County. The only other counties organized in 1864 were Beaverhead, Jefferson, Deer Lodge, and Missoula. Chouteau County was in the process of organizing.

Judicial districts were outlined and county of-

DENNIS J. CWIDAK

KEN SIEVERT

Above: *Montana's first newspaper, Virginia City's* Montana Post, *had its first printing in August 1864—960 copies at 50¢ each.*
Left: *Rustic, yet refined. The lancet Gothic windows of the* Montana Post *print shop reflect the details of more monumental structures in the eastern United States and in Europe, an indication of the town's early commitment to permanence.*

This Virginia City hotel later became the Madison.

ficers commissioned, and Edgerton set a general election for October 24 to choose territorial representatives and a delegate to the U.S. Congress.

The basically transient population of the area took little interest in developing the territory; most just wanted to "make their pile" and go home. With an election in the works, however, community spirit came to the fore, with a vengeance.

The president had appointed a Republican (Unionist) to govern a territory where a slight, but solid, majority of the population was Democrat. There were moderate and extreme factions within each party to further complicate things, as well as a great number of "openly declared Secessionists."

Many of the residents of the territory had purposely left the war far behind. There were dissenters, deserters, and veterans in the Gulch. Most carried guns, along with strong opinions, and were used to "self-government."

The issues of the Civil War dominated the campaign and the election. Thomas Dimsdale, the strongly Unionist *Montana Post* editor, fanned the smoldering animosity into flames at every opportunity. Battle lines were drawn and Edgerton's task of pulling the sides together to form a "more perfect" territory loomed large.

The October election, greased by drinks and encouragement to "vote often," provided the territory with a divided legislative assembly; the House was Democrat and the Council was Unionist. Democrat Samuel McLean was elected to serve as the territorial "voice" in Washington, defeating Unionist Wilbur F. Sanders.

The First Legislative Assembly of the Territory of Montana came together in Bannack on December 12, 1864, and for two months they crafted rudimentary laws to govern the territory, some 108 pieces of legislation. They created nine counties, divided the territory into three judicial districts and vested the judicial power in a full range of courts. (The Historical Society of Montana was incorporated during this first session.)

There were, in addition to general laws, special measures designed to meet the needs of the people and the times. Those included laws to prevent counterfeiting of gold dust and nine special acts for marital separation. The granting of charters to private enterprises ultimately drew a denunciation from the U.S. Congress.

The lawmakers were also charged with the responsibility of selecting a territorial capital. With visions of public buildings, government payrolls, and the general stabilizing effect of being the seat of a government, Bannack, Nevada City, and Virginia City vied for the position. The act naming Virginia City was approved February 7, 1865, subject to change only by a vote of the people. That proviso allowed a series of attempts, beginning in 1867, to wrest the seat of territorial government from Virginia City.

The difficult session ended with a long list of accomplishments, and possibly a longer list of unfinished business, much to the frustration of Edgerton, who compared working with the strongly divided legislature to dealing with the mounting Indian problems.

The Democrats were less than kind in their review of the Governor's performance—in 1867, the legislature changed the name of

TOM DIETRICH

Alder Gulch in autumn attire.

Edgerton County, created in the first session, to Lewis and Clark County.

CAPITAL CITY

At the time of the Alder Gulch gold discovery in May of 1863, there wasn't a house in Madison County; nor was there any government. As a part of Idaho Territory, which did not convene its first legislature until the following December, the area was technically not under the jurisdiction of any government.

On the day claims were staked, the Fairweather Mining District was established to protect the interests of the miners. Residents of the district then elected a sheriff, a judge, and a recorder; thus a miners' court became the first government for the Gulch.

The phenomenal growth of the political system nearly matched that of the population. At the end of 1864, with the population hovering somewhere between ten and fifteen thousand, Madison County was thrust headlong into political affairs.

Virginia City was incorporated under the laws of Montana in the winter of 1863–64. It was the only community in the whole territory which had the "blessings" of a municipal government.

Even the name of the community has its roots in politics. When the 320-acre townsite was recorded in June of 1863, the name Varina appeared on the records. Since the name was in honor of "arch-traitor" Jefferson Davis's wife, it seems an unsympathetic mining court "judge" summarily changed the name to Virginia.

Less than two years later, Virginia City was in full political bloom. She had the "blessings" of not only city and county governments, but also had succeeded in becoming the capital. The *Montana Post* proudly announced, "Capital of Montana Territory—*de lege* as well as *de facto*"—by law as well as in fact. President Andrew Johnson chose Civil War hero and fellow Union Democrat Thomas Francis Meagher as Territorial Secretary. The long-awaited secretary arrived in September 1865.

Governor Edgerton made some perfunctory introductions, and with little in the line of instructions, promptly turned the reins of government over to Meagher, as acting governor. Citing personal reasons and the need to take care of Montana's interests, Edgerton headed for Washington, neither resigning nor requesting leave, and promptly lost his post. While abandoning his post was likely reason enough for dismissal, the fact that President Johnson held little respect for Radical (also called Black) Republicans ultimately cost him his position.

Thomas Meagher, oft referred to as the Acting One, was to usher in one of the most chaotic periods in the history of Montana government. Meagher charged into the angry political situation in Virginia City and the territory, just as he had charged into fame as an organizer and commanding general of New York's Irish Brigade during the Civil War.

In the beginning, the Union Democrat seemed able to work with both political parties, but the acting governor shifted loyalty a little too freely to maintain good relations with both sides.

Meagher ultimately sided with the Democrats, who in addition to being a voting majority, were also heavily Irish. When he realized he had the power to do so, he called for an extraordinary session. Lawmakers gathered in Virginia City on March 5, 1866, and for two months hammered out legislation to keep the Territory running.

Democrats had been considering the advantages of seeking statehood. They were, after all,

MONTANA HISTORICAL SOCIETY

GEORGE WUERTHNER

in the majority and wanted the additional control that statehood would provide. Although the territory didn't have a large enough population to warrant statehood, the Democrats convinced Meagher to call for a Constitutional Convention, since it was necessary to submit a constitution to the U. S. Congress with an application for statehood.

Overshadowed by the concurrent legislative session, the convention never really got off the ground. The state constitution, produced in only six days by a spotty delegation, was lost; the carrier insisted he delivered it into the hands of the printer, but the printer claimed never to have seen it.

In the winter of 1867, Meagher convened the legislature again, which served to keep the political pots boiling. Republicans said that the special sessions were illegal and demanded that all the actions performed by the lawmakers be thrown out.

Some relief from the disorder came in October when Green Clay Smith was appointed to succeed Sidney Edgerton as territorial governor. His arrival prior to Meagher's special session gave him the opportunity to work with the Legislature. Although lawmakers responded well to the evenhanded Smith, the inherent problems of the territory were deep and wide. Tax collecting in the large, sparsely populated territory proved difficult. Funding issues and appointments to federal positions for the territory met with indifference, to the point of negligence, by the U.S. Congress. Conflict between immigrants and the natives was increasing; citizens were demanding protection, and the strongly divided legislature finally agreed on at least one thing—to send Smith back to Washington to help resolve the conflicts.

Once again Montana was left in the hands of T.F. Meagher. Once again the results were disastrous. The smell of battle was in the air. Reports of Indian depredations increased and the Fighting Irishman requested permission to raise a volunteer army to protect the citizens of the Bozeman Valley. The call for action intensified when John Bozeman was killed by Indians; Meagher answered the call. Gaining somewhat tenuous permission, he set out to make the area safe. His army encountered few

Indians, however, and despite efforts to produce some conflict, none materialized. He did succeed in exciting the tribes, as well as running up a debt of $1.1 million.

Governor Smith, in the meantime, discovered that one of his major problems had accompanied him to Washington. W.F. Sanders, one of the most outspoken Radical Republicans of the territory, had been sent to Washington to convince Congress to wipe the actions of Meagher's "bogus" sessions from the books. Despite Smith's efforts to the contrary, the Republican-controlled Congress responded by doing just that. This action removed many necessary laws, and added even more fuel to the political fires of the territory.

Governor Smith returned to Virginia City and called for another legislative session, to replace the laws erased by Congress. He also had the responsibility of cleaning up the situation created by the "Indian campaign" initiated by Meagher.

Meagher's colorful political career came to an abrupt end in July of 1867. After a trip to Camp Cook to obtain arms, he stopped at Fort Benton. While there, he accepted an invitation for a short ride on a steamboat. On his return, showing signs of a "disturbed mental condition," he was encouraged to retire to a stateroom. Thomas Francis Meagher was never seen again. His body was never recovered, although the river was carefully searched. Whatever the cause of his apparent death—suicide, accident, or foul play—he was mourned by many, cursed by some, and he left a colorful chapter in the history of Montana. General Meagher lives on, however, leading the charge, as a statue in front of the Capitol in Helena.

Meagher's death left the Territory once again short a Secretary, and again without access to federal funds. The Fourth Legislative Assembly, held in Virginia City in the winter of 1867, created Meagher County. It also designated Deer Lodge as the site for the Territorial prison, and acted on the incorporation of the City of Helena.

From then until 1870, Montana saw three governors come and go. Benjamin F. Potts, appointed in 1870, would serve fourteen years and at last stabilize territorial government. He also would attend the capital's departure from Virginia City.

No building was ever erected specifically for territorial government functions in Virginia City, even though a plot of land had been set aside for it. When the first legislature convened in 1866, the Council met on the second floor of a billiard hall, and the House met on the upper level of Stonewall Hall over a saloon. Territorial offices were located in Content Corner, also on a second floor. Upper levels of saloons, stores, and billiard halls were used for later sessions as well; at least a dozen different locations were used to house district courts.

Residents took great delight in ridiculing the legislature with mock sessions. A visitor to the community in 1867 commented, "The legislature is also running, and is one of the standard amusements of the city."

The question of the location of the capital surfaced in 1867 and was put to a vote of the populace, as required by the first legislative session. Although Helena was growing rapidly, Virginia City retained its position.

In 1869, the now-thriving Helena demanded another vote on the capital issue. The results of the election were destroyed by a fire, eliciting all manner of accusations, and again Virginia City emerged victorious. Helena continued to press, however, and the third election, held in 1874, offered the voters two choices: "for, or against, Helena." There were many irregularities in this election as well, with votes casually thrown out or labeled as fraudulent. The controversy was finally settled by the Montana Supreme Court, which ruled in favor of Helena.

The *Montana Post,* true to its style, reported on the move of the capital:

> ...the last remains and remnants of the moving Capital of Montana Territory passed down Wallace Street on a couple of Murphy freight wagons. It was an indifferent lot of old second-hand chairs, tables and three-legged stools, and might, if exposed at public auction, find a purchaser in some poor devil about to commit premature matrimony. Not another soul in the wide world would dream of buying it.

Facing page, top: *The Executive Building in Content Corner pictured before 1875, when the territorial capital moved from Virginia City to Helena.*
Bottom: *Legislative sessions were held on the top floors of saloons, stores, and billiard halls.*

This page: *Virginia City's Dance & Stuart Store was the site of the first meeting of the Montana Historical Society, in 1865.*

Facing page: *"Social City" band of the 1870s. There were balls and dances for almost every occasion.* MONTANA HISTORICAL SOCIETY

GEORGE WUERTHNER PHOTOS

The Social City

While politics divided the residents of Alder Gulch, it introduced an excitement that was eagerly embraced by the residents. A political rally, preceded by a torch-light parade, attracted large crowds to the social scene on the dusty streets and was a welcome break after a week of mining. Campaigns and elections also meant free drinks for voters.

Box- or wagon-mounted lobbyists shouted opinions, or politicians called out assurances, from the corners of Wallace Street. Eloquence and oratorical skills were important to attract a crowd, but volume was an absolute necessity in order to drown out the sounds of some of the other pastimes of the "Social City."

Fraternal organizations not only provided numerous social benefits to members, but began working for community "improvement" early in the history of Virginia City. The universal Square and Compass emblem announced the meeting place of the local Ancient and Free Accepted Masons. The *Montana Post* described an important aspect of the first Virginia City fraternal order: "In every clime a Mason may find a home, in every land a brother."

Organized in the winter of 1863, the brotherhood apparently extended to another organization formed about the same time—the Vigilantes. Paris Pfouts, a founding member of the local Masonic Lodge and Virginia City's first mayor, also served as president of the Vigilante Executive Committee. The lodge, largely made up of local businessmen, likely saw law and order as a high priority in community development.

The reigning cultural center for the territory, Virginia City gathered license fees from twenty-five hotels and eating houses, 73 liquor dealers and three dance houses in 1865. There were two theaters (of a sort) to entertain enthusiastic audiences. The Montana Theatre, which was later converted to a church, opened in 1864 in a log building; the People's Theatre opened two years later, in a billiards hall.

Con Orem's Champion Saloon was renamed the Melodeon Hall in 1866, perhaps to reflect the additional, more refined offerings of vaudeville and plays, some of which provided parts for local talent.

Orem's interest in "center stage" extended beyond the theater; he was one of the combatants in perhaps the longest "bare-knuckle" prizefight on record. Prizefights were another of the diversions popular in mining camps. On January 2, 1865, before a capacity crowd at Leviathon Hall, John Condle Orem—age 29, weighing in at 138 pounds and standing five feet six and a half inches—entered the ring to face Hugh O'Neil—age 34, 190 pounds, and standing five feet eight and a half inches. The match was "catch weights" and was fought according to London Prize

DENNIS J. CWIDAK

Virginia City's local lodge of the Ancient and Free Accepted Masons was organized in 1863. The brotherhood extended to another organization founded about the same time—the Vigilantes.

Ring rules, with the winner to take the purse and a certain amount of prestige. The fight ended in a draw—185 rounds, and three hours and five minutes later. The blow-by-blow account was recorded by Orem's friend, "the little professor," Thomas Dimsdale, and filled six columns of the January 7, 1865 edition of the *Montana Post.* Dimsdale's' literary prowess rose to the occasion with such anatomical cryptics as "tatoe trap," "knowledge box," "bread basket," and "olfactory department" to describe the punishment that caused the "ruby" to flow and "flushed the vermillion." Orem engaged in other prizefights; however, his interests increasingly returned to entertainment.

Well-known producer, actor, and director John S. Langrishe and his troupe of nine presented their varied repertoire at the People's Theater during the fall and winter seasons of 1867 and 1868. Patrons flocked to the unpainted building, and sitting on rough log benches, escaped to the fantasy on the small stage, away from the realities of the gold camp. Interestingly, audiences were smaller for comedies and farces than for melodramas or spectacles. The more serious fare, that which brought tears to the "manly eyes," was particularly well received. As an indication of the level of appreciation, Virginia City men presented one actress with a gift of a twenty-ounce gold nugget!

While the theater usually drew a respectable crowd, it was no competition for the saloons and dance halls. The hurdy-gurdy halls, where patrons could dance with one of the girls for a dollar in "dust," were extremely popular. The girls received half of the take for their efforts, and did well financially, much better than the miners who worked for wages.

Dancing was the rage in Virginia City and popular with nearly everyone, and not limited to the hurdy-gurdies. There were at least two dancing schools, appropriate for respectable citizens, which taught the fine art of the waltz, quadrille, and other current favorites. Dance instructors also traveled to outlying mining districts to prepare miners for leisure times. Virginia City was noted for its balls and dances for every occasion. With church and funerals

GARRY WUNDERWALD

Evidence of Virginia City's past life.

obvious exceptions, a dance followed nearly every meeting in the community.

As the population declined, the hurdy-gurdies turned (even more) to less-respectable activities as a source of income, and were forced to close by 1866.

But Lady Virginia danced on. Saloons continued to do a brisk business, and the west end of Wallace Street became home to the "Red Light District" in Virginia City. In *Frontier Woman,* Mary Ronan recalls childhood memories of the "Ladies" who lived there:

> ...a certain class of women whom I heard called "Fancy Ladies" because of their gaudy dress, so different from that of the ladies who were our friends. They were always to be seen either walking up and down or clattering along on horseback or in hacks. Sometimes one was glimpsed through a window lounging in a dressing gown and puffing a cigarette. They were so in evidence that I felt no curiosity about them. I knew that they were not "good women." I did not analyze why.

Competition for the ladies was brisk enough to cause much of the fighting that erupted in the saloons and on the streets, which was another favorite, though not particularly social, pastime.

Montana Post editor Thomas Dimsdale worked hard to keep the citizenry informed of social activities, including those in the "Celestial Regions," referred to by most others as Chinatown. Dimsdale, gave credit to the "weaker vessels" in a disturbance that was "...kicked up in the locality sacred to the residence of the Almond eyed portion of our population. The Chinamen began it; and the Chinawoman (the lovely musk scented pinks of the Flowery Kingdom) ended it."

Serenading was a popular activity for young men, who would gather in the spring to learn old love songs and croon at the doors of the crude cabins on balmy summer nights. Courting was rampant in Virginia City, and the *Montana Post* seemed to take great pleasure in clearing up "episodes which never fail to give the tongue of gossip increased glibness."

Many of the miners were single, or had families back home, which could explain why the first Legislative Assembly passed nine laws regarding separation. Later sessions devoted considerable time to both separation and divorce laws.

Marriages received nearly equal time in the press. When D.W. Tilton married Miss Lizzie D. Day, the *Post* reported that he had: "wisely concluded to double his joys and halve his troubles."

Father Joseph Giorda provided the first religious services in the community in the late fall of 1863. Miners, for the most part, respected the Sabbath by not working. It was not for purposes of churchgoing, however, much to the chagrin of the clergy. Services were not particularly well attended until the community attracted more women, families, and professional people. St. Mary's Catholic Church appeared in 1867, in the converted Montana Theater building. Baptist, Methodist, and Episcopal religions followed, also using "found" places. In 1867 the Methodists built the first real church edifice. Bishop Daniel S. Tuttle finished building the original St. Paul's Episcopal church in 1868.

GEORGE WUERTHNER

In St. Paul's Episcopal Church. The parish was organized in Virginia City in 1867, with a wooden structure completed in 1868. The stone church was built in 1902.

Those mining for wages worked from sunrise to sunset; they were generally paid on Saturday evening. Saturday night and Sunday found Virginia City teeming with activity. Sunday was the day to get cleaned up, replenish supplies, make repairs, pick up news from home, and socialize.

In November of 1865 a literary club for young men, the Lyceum, was formed, and the second floor of Stonewall Hall over the Gem Saloon became a reading and meeting room for members. The *Post* supported the establishment of the Lyceum as a system which "engenders a relish for intellectual improvement."

Schools appeared as families began to immigrate to the rough new country, or as a result of the aforementioned courting. The earliest were subscription schools, with classes generally held in the home of the teacher. Thomas Dimsdale opened such a school in Virginia City in 1863 prior to becoming editor of the *Post.* He charged $1.75 per week for each student. There were also two "singing schools" in Virginia City.

The first legislature provided the means for public education in the territory by authorizing counties to levy taxes for schools. Madison County quickly took advantage, and the first public school in the territory opened in Virginia City in 1866.

For the more sports minded, the city inaugurated a skating rink in the winter of 1868. Possibly winter sports got a little out of hand, as the town council was forced to outlaw snowballing.

The adventurous reported a strange land of geysers, unusual formations, hot bubbling springs, and other freaks of nature, the first introduction of tourism to the Social City. By the early 1870s, Virginia City was organizing excursions and became a point of departure to the astonishing Yellowstone region, some 125 miles away. Residents were singing "I Want to Go Where the Geysers Go." The trip into the extremely rugged, roadless area, with the potential for Indian conflict, was not for the faint-hearted.

Nathaniel P. Langford, the first collector of Internal Revenue for Montana Territory, and one of the Vigilantes, was also a member of the official, nine-member military and scientific Yellowstone Expedition of 1870. Others who were willing to brave the dangers included Cornelius Hedges, who was so inspired by the wonders that he proposed setting the area aside as a national park.

When lawmakers gathered in Virginia City for the seventh session of the territorial legislature in 1871, they urged the U.S. Congress to set apart the Yellowstone area "...to be devoted to public use, resort and recreation for all time to come." Montana Territory's Congressional delegate, William H. Clagett, drafted the park bill and introduced it to the U.S. Congress. N.P. Langford and Dr. William Hayden, who drew the boundaries, lobbied the nation's lawmakers with photographs and specimens of the area. The bill setting aside Yellowstone National Park was signed into law on March 1, 1872.

Langford—"some were wont to call him 'National Park' Langford"— became the first superintendent of the Park.

GEORGE WUERTHNER

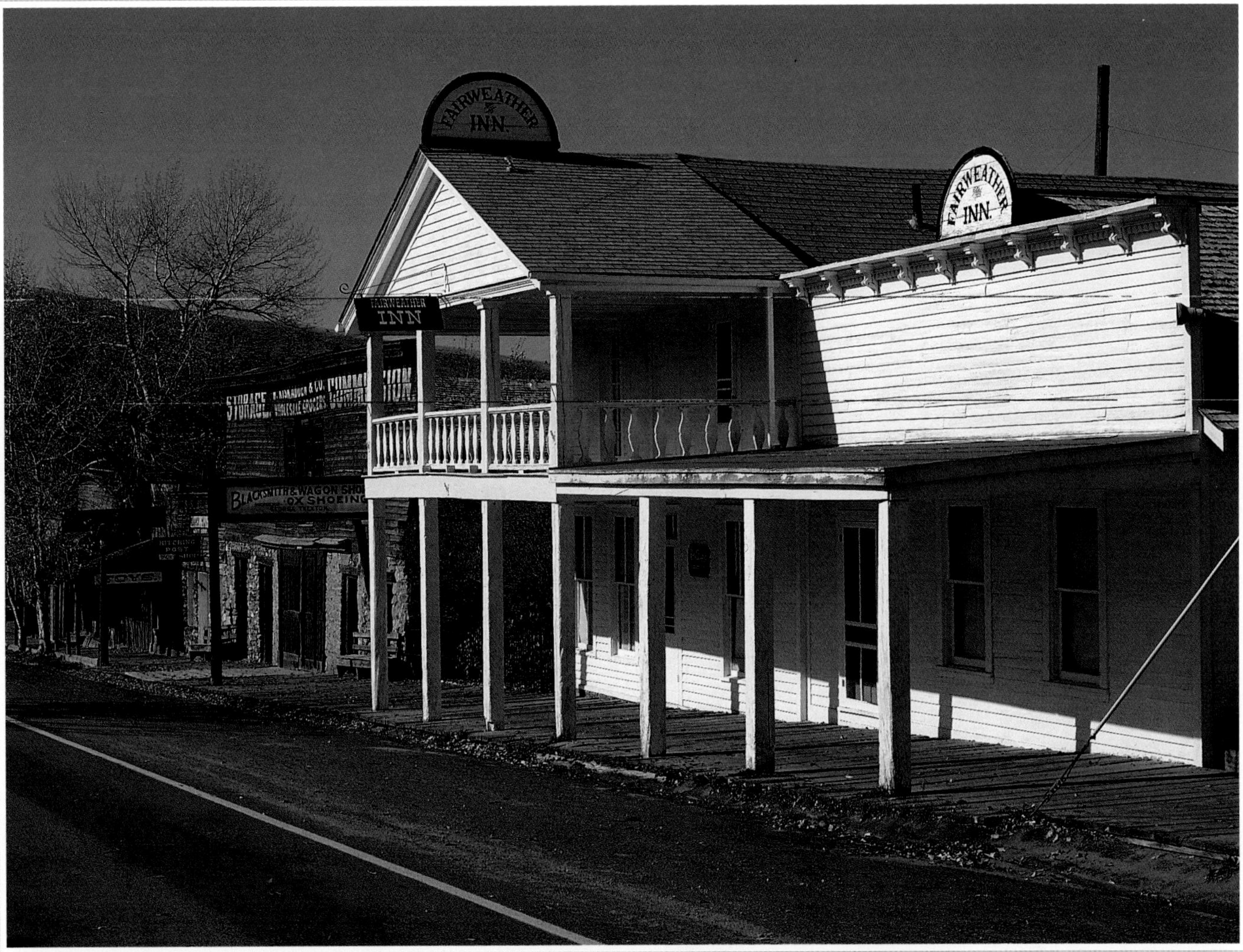

KENT & CHARLENE KRONE

The Fairweather Inn opened in Virginia City in 1946 and it continues to offer a fitting atmosphere for a journey back in time.

GEORGE WUERTHNER

GEORGE WUERTHNER

JOHN REDDY

Above: *McGovern's Store.*
Top right: *Virginia City with all the trimmings.*
Right center: *The spice of life.*
Far right: *Peace restored to the Gulch.*
Right: *To find out why, see page 16.*

WAYNE SCHERR

WAYNE SCHERR

JOHN REDDY

WAYNE SCHERR

JOHN REDDY

Above: *Cents of times long past.*
Top left: *Virginia City's attention to detail.*
Left: *Oliver and Conover established the first stage line to Salt Lake City in 1863, but coachman Ben Holladay started a rival line with lower fares and dominated the business until he sold out to Overland–Wells Fargo in 1866.*

Brief Glory

Virginia was putting on "city airs" by the summer of 1864. Substantial buildings were going up, quickly replacing the temporary mining camp structures. The roughest elements of the population had been eliminated by the Vigilantes early in the year and people continued to crowd into the area. In the evening, with candles or lanterns lighting the openings of small cabins, the area took on the appearance of a vast, "fourteen-mile city."

In August 1864 a *Montana Post* report said, "One hundred buildings are being erected each week in Virginia City and its environs."

Governor Edgerton, visiting the same month, remarked, "The growth of our beautiful city appeared the work of magic."

News of gold strikes in other areas of the territory spread in that same year and began to draw miners away from Alder Gulch and off to the camps of Emigrant, Confederate, and Last Chance. The discovery in Last Chance Gulch was to have a profound impact on Virginia City. It soon resulted in the founding of Helena, and within a year's time, it was clear that Helena was there to stay.

Commerce was briefly stimulated by the

establishment of Helena, as several enterprising Virginia City businesses opened branches in the new "boom" town. Three stage lines facilitated commerce, as well as considerable socialization, between what the *Montana Post* described as "...the center of wealth, population, and intelligence of the territory" and the rough new mining camp of Helena.

Virginia City was maturing. Although still very much a frontier mining town, she remained the active center of county and territorial governments, as well as serving the social and commercial needs for a large section of the territory.

In 1865, with the announcement that seven substantial stone buildings had been erected, and four more "well advanced," the *Post* noted:

> The streets are rapidly losing the air of "sudden inspiration" so common to mining towns and cities. There are method and design in the structures recently put up and in a short time our young city will present as creditable an aspect as many an older place.

Virginia was dressing for a ball that was nearly over.

By the late 1860s, Virginia City was home to a diminishing mining population. Approximately 2,000 people remained; while many still mined, others turned to various trades and professions. The community changed in terms of ethnic diversity as well—the first Chinese citizens were noted in 1865.

Drinks, politics, and yellow journalism continued to flow in Virginia City; the "Acting One," Thomas Meagher, kept things stirred up for the territory until his death in 1867. The later administrations of James Tufts, James M. Ashley, and Benjamin F. Potts, while quieter, still provided plenty of political action in the community. The 1870 census, however, recorded only 867 residents in Virginia City, and one-third of the population was Chinese.

Virginia City was resurveyed and platted in 1868 by John L. Corbett. The nearly 580-acre plat indicated Capitol Square, a 300-foot by 450-foot site selected by W.F. Sanders and R.B. Parrot of Virginia City, and George Christman of Bannack. Commissioned by the First Legislative Assembly in Bannack, the men were allowed ten dollars per day, and thirty cents per horseback mile to complete the task of selecting the site.

MONTANA HISTORICAL SOCIETY PHOTOS BOTH PAGES

Above: *The north side of Virginia City's Wallace Street in the 1920s.*

Facing page, top: *Elaborate homes—sometimes with unusual combinations of architectural styles—sprinkled throughout the community mark the evolution from mining camp to town.*
Bottom: *Masonic Hall. The museum on the right was once City Drug.*

Mining production never again approached the levels of 1863 to 1865. As the mining population continued its decline, businesses followed suit, relocating to more prosperous locales like Helena.

History was repeating itself in the territory, and in March of 1866, the *Montana Post* lamented:

> Most of the log houses in the crooked strip are empty, their owners gone to the Blackfoot country. The American miner is a migratory animal, who will always leave the certainty of $5 for the possibility of $20 per day.

The decline continued, particularly after Virginia City lost the territorial capital title in 1875. During her decade-long reign as the capital, Virginia City witnessed the administrations of four governors and two acting governors, numerous legislative sessions (two of them "bogus"), and saw the creation of the foundation upon which rests the government of the State of Montana.

There was an up side to the declining population and the loss of the capital. As Virginia

MONTANA HISTORICAL SOCIETY

The William Kiskadden & Co. Storage & Commission House was Vigilante headquarters, and later a livery stable and blacksmith shop. The "woody" in this 1948 photograph—still running twenty-five years later—belonged to Charles Bovey.

City grew smaller, its architecture grew more elaborate. Several large, prominent homes were built between 1880 and 1890. The city was filled with "respectable" people. There were churches, "quite good stores," a fine hotel, and—most important—the hospitality of the residents. Virginia City continued to serve the needs of a large trade area in southwestern Montana through the 1880s, and the new (1875) Madison County Courthouse provided steady activity and employment. A demand for silver created another brief mining boom.

By 1890, the population of Virginia City had dipped to 600, but Virginia City had become home to many, not just a place to "make a pile" and leave. Nestled in the crooked gulch, in an isolation forced by terrain and circumstances, Virginia City persevered.

Mining picked up with the advent of the dredge boat early in the new century. The dredges continued to "ravish" the gulch until $7.5 million in gold was removed by 1922.

There were only 242 residents in the community when Humphrey's Gold Company, encouraged by the rising price of the precious commodity, came in the 1930s. The company purchased a local hotel and converted it to a boarding house for its miners. The high gold prices also encouraged hard-rock mining in the hills, and two mills were built. Virginia City once again attracted miners and their families.

Some former residents returned during this period of national depression, partly because of the low cost of living in the self-sufficient community. Miners could practice their craft on their own claims and make more money than public works programs paid. To those without claims, the larger mining companies offered a chance for employment.

Humphrey's dredge and payroll were gone by 1937, along with a portion of the population. By this time, many of the buildings in Virginia City, already over seventy years old, were deteriorating. Abandoned buildings were torn down and the materials used for other construction or for firewood. Fire destroyed a number of buildings in 1937, and a hotel was demolished as a safety hazard. The buildings in the nearby camps of Nevada City, Junction, and Central City had been demolished by the dredging operations.

The 1940s were hard on Virginia City as men left for service in World War II. Probably for the first time, there was no mining in the gulch. The U. S. government shut down mining when it labeled precious-metal mining a nonessential industry and issued the Gold Mine Closing Order of 1942.

DENNIS J. CWIDAK

Dredging was the preferred gold extraction method from 1897 through 1922.

FREE AND NOT-SO-FREE GOLD

Alder Gulch yielded an immense amount of gold during the discovery years, and the *Montana Post* reported another $30 million produced from 1865 to 1867, and almost as much during the transition from placer to quartz mining before the end of the decade. (In placer—*plass*-er—mining "free," or loose, gold in streams is captured; in quartz, or hard-rock, mining the ore is recovered from underground by blasting.)

Virginia City gold was purer and of better color than most, and it typically brought around $18 per ounce at the scales—about $1.50 per ounce more than the average rate. Although total production was less than that of South Dakota's Homestake, Cripple Creek, the Comstock Lode at Virginia City, Nevada, or the central California "mother lode" near Sutter's mill, Virginia City, Montana ranked high on the scale of gold-producing areas.

There are those who attribute the financing of the Civil War to Virginia City and Montana gold. It is known that the gold contributed to the founding of Creighton University in Omaha because of E. Creighton's presence in the Gulch. Harvard University assumed control of one of the major dredge companies in the Gulch at the turn of the twentieth century, another indicator of the wealth of the area.

The original discovery at Virginia City was of the easily extracted placer gold—the dream of the nomadic and, usually poor, miner. Armed with a greater knowledge of practical science than he is usually credited with, the miner could simply wash the unencumbered dust or nuggets from the gravel and earth. If the discovery was sizeable, he could build a sluice from a few boards to wash the earth away from the gold. The rocker and the long-tom were sluice variations that rocked to stir up the earth. The principles of placering eventually grew into the more sophisticated and mechanized methods of hydraulic mining and dredging. The flume companies washed away entire hillsides using water pressure; dredge boats followed the mineral-laden stream beds up-channel as the large gravel-eating barges first created their own pond, and then scoured the perimeter, depositing the waste overburden in rows of gravel piles along the route. Both of these processes were used in Virginia City and the scars are still visible today.

Water is essential to all of the variations of placer mining—panning, sluicing, hydraulic mining, or floating dredge boats—and Alder Gulch had a free-flowing stream, but not always enough water. The Virginia City Water Company formed early to assure fair dispensation to the miners. In 1868 during the exceptionally dry spring, surveyor J.L. Corbett was engaged to develop a plan that would divert part of the Madison River across the range to the upper part of the Gulch; however, June rains eclipsed execution of the plan. It may have been providential—mining production declined that year, and by August

Facing page, far right: *The stream of Alder Gulch was described by the Virginia City Mining Company as "The Greatest Natural Sluice in America."*
Top: *Relic in Nevada City. Alder Gulch had a free-flowing stream, but not always with enough water to go around.*
Bottom: *Along the Ruby River above the Ruby Reservoir.*

the *Montana Post* reported that the Water Company was in debt.

Then there is the not-so-free gold that is chemically, thermally, or mechanically bonded in matrices of quartz, igneous rock, chlorides, and sulfides. Extracting the gold from these various ores required ponderous machinery, sophisticated chemical treatment, often greater penetration into the earth to acquire the ore, or a combination of the above. In lode mining, the miner might find the gold, but would have to sell the claim to those who could afford to develop it. This also holds true today.

Widespread placer mining as practiced by the independent miner generally ended at the conclusion of the Civil War, to be replaced by hydraulics, dredging, or lode process mining. In Virginia City, post-war mining changed over time to process mining upstream from the town, and dredging downstream. Prospectors knew that the closer to the mountains the bigger the nuggets, and the nuggets were largest up Alder Gulch near Summit. The upper gulch characteristically had less free gold, but had more ore bodies that were thought to be the source of the placer gold below.

Improvements in explosives during the war also contributed to further development of ore mines upstream from Virginia City. Mills were constructed at the Oro Cache, Grizzly Gulch, Lucas, Seneca Falls, and the Kearsarge mines. Ore mining persisted in the upper gulch until 1876 when most of the machinery was silenced, although a new era of production started at the Kennett lode in 1897 and large-scale redevelopment began at the Kearsarge in Summit in 1901.

The new Kearsarge boasted sixty stamps in the mill to pulverize the ore, and used amalgam concentration and cyanidation for the extraction of gold. The new Kearsarge was the scene of Virginia City's most tragic mining disaster, just as it was beginning to implement full-scale operation of its new capabilities. In the early morning hours of November 6, 1903, a temporary construction building above the tunnel caught fire, trapping the four men on the 11 P.M. shift underground. Unable to rescue the miners via the main tunnel, the mine superintendent and five volunteers attempted to reach them through an intersecting shaft. The fire spread back into the timbering of the main tunnel and generated enough poisonous gas to overcome four of the volunteers and, unfortunately, the four miners who were coming up out of the workings, unaware of the scene at the surface of the mine. Eight men died, including the mine superintendent. The last two volunteers to enter the shaft, warned by the others below, made it back to safety.

The Kearsarge rebounded from the disaster. By 1904 it was the largest producer in Virginia City; a 1914 U.S. government survey of the mining districts reported that the mine contained 8,000 feet of tunnels that reached to a depth of 400 feet below the surface.

Downstream, dredging became the preferred method of extraction, beginning in 1897 and continuing through 1922. The German Bar Placer Mining Company and McKay–Conrey Placer Mining Company pioneered the efforts by building dredges on-site. The steam dredge *Maggie A. Gibson* was brought to the gulch from Bannack, rebuilt in 1897–98, and operated for five years. Two electric stacker dredges were pressed into service by 1908, and a third mammoth electric dredge (the largest in the world) was built in 1910. The dredge activity prompted the building of the workers' town of Ruby and the introduction of electricity to the area—furnished by the Madison Electric Company.

The dredge boats have long gone, but the ponds still can be seen from Virginia City to Laurin. Panning for placer gold is pursued by only a few, and there have been sporadic bursts of lode mining since the turn of the century, but none of past magnitude. Not yet anyway. Nevertheless, Virginia City continues to devote a fair amount of attention to the subject of mining. It is always a topic of conversation at the watering holes. Geologists and attorneys from distant places frequent the courthouse researching mining claims. There seems to be a perpetual activity of exploration or development, and current claims along the Gulch are as zealously guarded as they were in 1863.

DENNIS J. CWIDAK

BEVERLY R. MAGLEY

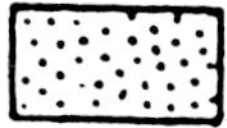

RECENT ALLUVIUM

BOZEMAN LAKE BEDS (TERTIARY)

ANDESITE

BASALT

APLITE

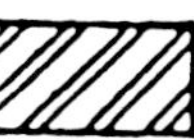

PRE-CAMBRIAN GNEISS, SCHIST, AND MARBLE

THE "SLUICEBOX"

DENNIS J. CWIDAK

In Nevada City. Maps of the period show many buildings in Virginia City labeled "Chinese laundry."

THE CHINESE

The area around Virginia City has borne witness to a rich diversity of culture through the passage of time—hunters and gatherers, nomadic Indian peoples, trappers and explorers, and miners of nearly every description and background. In Virginia City, the nomadic life was replaced with agrarian settlement and tourism, replete with permanent structures and a (sometimes) definable social structure. Included in that march of many to the area are the easily-identified and little-understood Chinese, who arrived during the territorial years.

Overpopulation, poverty, and political turmoil had been reasons for leaving their Far East homeland. American's natural resources and opportunity for better lives drew them first to California.

Most of the Chinese came from the maritime province of Kwangtung along the southeast China Coast, with the largest numbers leaving their native shores between 1852 and 1854. Many of those seeking passage to America used the "credit ticket" system—the barter of labor for travel—arranged by six Chinese companies in California.

The Chinese typically followed after the first wave of activity had run its course in the mining camps, and their entry into Montana was no exception. Often prohibited by law from owning claims, they traditionally reworked abandoned sites. Many miners associated the arrival of Chinese as an indication that the "colors" were about "played out," and the miners resented them. The *Walla-Walla Statesman* reported Chinese at Virginia City in 1866, and the *Montana Post* reported on Chinese activities in Alder Gulch and Last Chance Gulch as early as 1865. The 1870 census showed 1,949 Chinese in the fledgling territory. Primarily concentrated in Virginia City, Helena, and Butte, the Chinese numbered about 2,000 until the beginning of the twentieth century. At the time of the 1920 census, only 900 remained.

Virginia City saw the largest influx around 1870 when Chinese companies bought the rights to rework some claims in the gulch, an effort they pursued for the next twenty-five years. The 1880 census listed 265 Chinese in Alder Gulch; in 1879, neighboring Adobetown reportedly housed more Chinese than white residents.

China Point, near Beaverhead Rock, got its name when eight ill-prepared Chinese lost their lives in a sub-zero Montana blizzard while en route to Virginia City.

In Virginia City, as elsewhere, the work of the Chinese complemented the work of the first rush of miners who now were leaving. With an understanding that "many hands make light work," and culturally steeped in the value of frugality, the Chinese continued to recover gold, slowing the decline of the mining town. They also did work that the miners were allergic to, such as laundry and domestic chores. Sanborn Insurance Company maps of the period show numerous buildings in Virginia City labeled "Chinese laundry."

The businesses the Chinese supported, and the businesses they created, added to the tax bases of the territorial camps. In the 1880s, significant numbers of Chinese provided the labor needed to bring the railroad into Montana and the northwest.

The Chinese miners brought their traditional social orders and organizations with

DENNIS J. CWIDAK

them, but not their families. In 1870, only 123 of the 1,949 Chinese recorded were female, and in 1890, only 59 of 2,532. Adherence to their cultural ways was perhaps intensified by the lack of family—many spent their time engaged in activities at the Chinese Masonic Lodge or at the prestigious Joss House (temple), which in Virginia City was located at the lower end of Wallace Street. They kept secret the internal workings and leadership of the Chinese ritualistic orders and organizations, a practice that raised suspicion among their white neighbors.

Initially, Montana territorial law treated the immigrants fairly, but as national sentiment turned against the Chinese in the 1870s, Montana law also began to reflect a different attitude. New restrictions on, or exclusion from, ownership of mines, tax disincentives, and social nonacceptance took their toll. The workers from the ancient civilization quietly retraced their footsteps from the mining camp, leaving little evidence of their years of toil.

MONTANA HISTORICAL SOCIETY

Above: *Chinese store in Nevada City.*
Left: *Chinese Temple at the lower end of Wallace Street in Virginia City. There was also a Chinese Masonic Lodge.*

ELLEN SIEVERT

NEW RUSH TO THE GULCH

When Charles Argalis Bovey graduated from Phillips Academy in Massachusetts in 1924, he was "prepared" for Yale, but the young man "with a stubborn chin and a poet's dreamy eye" entertained other notions. His education and his Minnesota family instilled in Charlie a keen interest in American history—particularly the history of the west.

Charlie convinced his father to let him go west to learn the flour milling business. His father was president of the Minneapolis-based Royal Milling Company, a subsidiary of Washburn Crosby Company, which later became General Mills. Charlie arrived in Montana in 1926, and went to work at the Royal Mill in Great Falls.

His interest in the milling business paled when he met and fell in love with Rachel Sue Ford, a third-generation Montanan, daughter and granddaughter of Cascade County pioneers. Her grandfather, Robert S. Ford, had driven some of the first cattle into Montana and was one of the earliest settlers in the Sun River Valley. He was also a founder of the Great Falls National Bank. Her father, Lee Ford, succeeded his father as president of the bank, which later became Norwest Bank.

Charlie and Sue were married in 1933. Charlie began a ranching career, raising wheat, purebred Hereford cattle, and sheep on the Sunnyside Ranch east of Great Falls.

It was during the early 1940s that Charles and Sue Ford Bovey first visited Virginia City. Both loved to travel, and as they motored around the state, Sue often read aloud from the Montana history books that were usually packed in the car. This practice was introduced by Charlie's older brother, and quickly became a family tradition—a tradition which fueled their interest in the state and its history.

They passed through wonderfully pungent sage country on that fateful first visit, rising into the foothills of the Tobacco Root Mountains, on the still gravel Highway 1, which had been bypassed years earlier by more modern transportation routes. The ranges of the Rocky Mountains created a dramatic 360-degree backdrop.

GREAT FALLS TRIBUNE

Left: *Charles and Sue Ford Bovey, Virginia and Nevada cities' best friends.*

Facing page: *Virginia City sheds the leaves from her trees and the tourists from her streets as she prepares for the quiet winter of an isolated community.*

Sue may have been recounting historic tales of Virginia City as they traveled, but both knew enough to be eager to see the place behind the colorful history. Charlie had been elected to the State House of Representatives in that fall of 1942, and maybe he just wanted to see where Montana government started.

They began to see remnants of the mining era as they neared Virginia City—small, rough log cabins, crumbling into the ground. There were huge piles of overturned rock left behind by the dredge boats that had "reworked" the gulch until 1937.

The "river cobble" trail along the highway led to a cluster of deserted buildings on the lower end of Wallace Street in Virginia City, which looked a lot like a dilapidated movie set, complete with boardwalks. Farther up the street was the bustle of a functioning business district.

In the 1940s, Virginia City was a community of fewer than 400 people, many still clinging to the hope of finding the "mother lode," while others carried on business as usual. That included demolition of some of the old buildings for public safety reasons or to reuse the building materials.

Many vestiges of the early 1860s remained, however; the largest collection of buildings was at the western edge of the community, while others were scattered throughout the townsite—and beyond—some still in use, others at risk.

Buildings constructed during the evolution from mining camp to town stood as evidence of that transition—proud masonry structures

KEN SIEVERT SKETCH

The east side of South Jackson in Virginia City.

and buildings displaying the later influences of Victorian architecture were sprinkled throughout the community.

The Boveys were particularly taken by the two-story Dudley Garage, which had opened as the Stonewall House Saloon in 1864. The upper level had provided the meeting room and library for the Virginia City Lyceum, and later served the Territorial House of Representatives when they first came together in the "extraordinary" session of 1866 called by Acting Governor Thomas Meagher.

Other buildings were beckoning as well, all displaying a proud past, but perhaps a dim future. The Boveys said, "We can't just let all this crumble away."

Back in Great Falls, Charlie contacted noted historian Joseph Kinsey Howard and others concerned about the potential loss of historic sites around the state. In the summer of 1944, they incorporated the nonprofit Historic Landmark Society of Montana and worked to build an organization dedicated to saving the state's valuable landmarks. The society boasted a membership of 371, including 24 life-time members. The society considered preserving such sites as the jail at Bannack, Fort Shaw, Fort Logan, and Saint Peter's Mission, in addition to buildings in Virginia City. They accomplished restoration work on a mill near Craig, put a roof on a fur trader's cabin near Loma, and in Virginia City purchased and rebuilt the badly burned Montana Post building, the site of the state's first newspaper. A 1948 issue of *Rocky Mountain Magazine* said that Charlie, as the Society's president, "...fired hundreds of members with his enthusiasm." Contributions and offers of labor poured in, and when more money was needed, which was often, he put in his own.

Charlie soon discovered it was expensive and time-consuming to bring in members while trying to keep up with the demands of organizing a statewide group. He figured he'd actually save money if he just put the dollars up himself. The Historic Landmark Society could then concentrate on projects in Virginia City. The Boveys ultimately donated money to the organization to purchase and preserve other buildings that had captured their imagination on their first trip to Virginia City.

In the fall of 1945, Charlie bought a small residence, "lock, stock and splinters," for one hundred dollars, likely more than it was worth for salvage. The modest building had been the home of Judge Henry Blake, who became U. S. Attorney for Montana Territory in 1869. Blake served in the legislature several terms and on the territorial Supreme Court in 1875. In 1889, he was elected first Chief Justice of the State of Montana. Charlie couldn't pass the building up, and the purchase triggered the notion that he could more readily save the historically significant, deteriorating structures if he bought them.

Following two terms in the House of Representatives, Charlie was elected to the state Senate in 1946, a seat he held for twenty years. His Great Falls ranching operations grew and prospered, and the Boveys continued to plow the profits into the preservation of Virginia City. They spent as much time as possible there, repairing and stabilizing buildings and hauling in "treasures" for display. Charlie said, "The fun of collecting anything is enhanced when one has a place where others can see and enjoy the collection; to lock it up in a dark shed accessible only to myself would give me little pleasure."

As word of the Bovey collection and restoration project spread, offers of old building materials, artifacts, vehicles, and even buildings were received from everywhere. People were always happy to get a few dollars for things they were going to throw away, and Charlie relished breathing new life into a relic of the past, whether it be a stagecoach, a building, or a music machine.

The Boveys scoured every corner of Montana, then "ransacked" the whole country for everything from old corsets to penny-arcade peep shows, "seeking relics which might bring the old mining town back to life." Virginia City residents couldn't see how the man from Great Falls, or even a group of people, could "...revive a whole town which had been on the downgrade for eighty years. But Bovey just stuck out his square chin and proceeded," said *Rocky Mountain Magazine.*

The Boveys had faith that folks would see the significance of what they were doing, and by the early 1950s, about 175,000 people were arriving annually in Virginia City to step into the 1860s. The Boveys had opened a Pandora's Box, however, as their interest in collecting had evolved to the point where they found themselves with the "headaches" of the restaurant, saloon, theater, and hotel businesses. They also had to provide housing for a growing summer staff, and they continued to buy and convert or add buildings throughout the community for that purpose.

GEORGE WUERTHNER

Those in Alder Gulch mining for wages usually got paid on Saturday evening for their gruelling sunrise-to-sunset workdays. Saturday night and Sunday found Virginia City miners replenishing supplies.

The historically raucous and never-say-die "Lady of Virginia" found a friend when she was discovered and courted by Charles Bovey—it was a love affair that would last over thirty years, until his death in 1978. He was often found working alongside masons, roofers, and carpenters, and quickly became a familiar sight to everyone in Virginia City. Residents looked on with amusement, and some skepticism, at the "junk-collecting" while the Boveys hauled in truckloads of collectibles and furnishings.

Even with the encouragement and support of many enthusiastic hands, by the late 1940s, Charlie realized that the preservation work at Virginia City was analogous to "chewing a tough steak"—the more that was accomplished, the bigger the job got. Research, acquisitions, management, exhibition, and stabilization required enormous effort and eventually swallowed the assets of two of the Boveys' working ranches, along with other personal investments.

Following the philosophy of "preservation without fresh paint," Charlie and Sue drew upon their exposure to places like Williamsburg, Virginia, and Henry Ford's Greenfield Village near Detroit, along with their own instincts, for guidance. Their pioneering efforts in preservation started twenty years before the milestone 1966 Historic Preservation Act, and nearly thirty years before the Department of Interior Standards that guide preservation work today.

Highway 287 was paved to Virginia City in 1948, and the Lady Virginia would dance on to become second only to the national parks as a state visitor attraction.

Formed in 1948 when Charles Bovey was seeking entertainment for a miners' convention, The Virginia City Players found a home in the converted Smith and Boyd Livery in 1949.

The People

While the buildings created the initial interest, it wasn't long before the gregarious Charlie Bovey discovered another of the community resources—its people. There were many residents with roots that extended back to the formative years of the camp, descendants of those to whom Virginia City became home. Among those were Harvey Romey (1901-1979) and Bob Gohn (1900-1986), who not only shared stories of their respective ancestors, but added some history of their own, and dedicated their lives to the town.

Harvey was a descendent of Lucien Romey, a Swiss gardener who arrived in 1863 and, among other things, is remembered for establishing Romey's gardens, which provided fresh produce for residents. Harvey ran the Pioneer Bar, and in the tradition of Western self-reliance, had acquired a variety of skills. For example, he would give haircuts in the barber shop in the front window of his saloon while the patron "sampled the malt."

Distinguished for his fun-loving sense of humor, Harvey would lighten life's burden with his storytelling. "A thousand lives were lost," he would proclaim, "when they tore down my seven-story hotel across the street." He would then explain to the amazed listener—who couldn't imagine such a catastrophe—that the lives were all "bedbugs."

Harvey's community service included serving as mayor of the town, as well as contributing his time and efforts to keeping the place vital during trying times. His idea of a vacation wasn't some far-away place, but a log cabin just up the gulch, near Highland.

Bob Gohn's grandfather was among the first 200 to arrive in the gulch, in 1863, and he was one of the Vigilante crew. Bob's father, George E. Gohn, was born in Virginia City in 1865, and there he stayed.

At age twenty, Bob lost his eyesight and part of his hearing in a blasting accident at the High-Up mine in Hungry Hollow in 1920. He spent the next two years at the School for the Deaf and Blind in Boulder, eventually going on to teach vocational classes while finishing his studies. Gohn returned to Virginia City during Prohibition, first to run the Anaconda Pool Hall, and later to operate The Little Club Bar. In the fall of 1929, Bob introduced "talking pictures" to Virginia City, playing to a full house. Before long, he was also hauling his projection equipment to Twin Bridges, Whitehall, Ennis, and Sheridan. Bob purchased Content Corner in 1943; in 1947 he left the movie business to devote full time to his store.

Bob's blindness was a surprise to many because he led such a normal, successful life. For example, one winter, folks dropping in to Bob's Territorial Bar and Sport Shop were surprised to find Bob laying a hardwood floor by himself.

Bob Gohn and Harvey Romey serve to exemplify the spirit of many residents who worked towards the "new rush to Virginia City"—after a period of observing. Many soon opened up their own camelback trunks to add to exhibits. The town's mayor, Jimmy Vanderbeck, owner of Rank's Drugstore, opened a museum in the basement of his store in the 1940s. The building, with a history of its own, was completed in 1865, by Paris Pfouts, the first mayor of the community and head of the Vigilantes.

Frank Carey, chairman of the Montana State Parks board at the time, was a resident who early caught the vision of preserving the town. He and Charlie Bovey spent "long, friendly hours beside a fire, pouring over old records." Then there was Zena Hoff, a Danish actress who had been "dumped" in Virginia City by her mining-engineer beau. Zena provided hard work and influence for the preservation effort in its formative years. She also retrieved the town's original streetlights from the dump. Her own home had been the house where Jack

Slade's wife supposedly kept her husband's body in an alcohol-filled coffin until it could be transported to Salt Lake City. With a reputation of serious crimes, Slade was hanged for a misdemeanor in March 1864.

It seemed that every building and every person had a story to tell, and as the history came out, so did the enthusiasm, inside and outside the community. It became necessary to provide lodging and other services for visitors, and the Fairweather Inn and the Wells Fargo Cafe were opened in 1946.

Entertainment came along in 1948 with the advent of the Virginia City Players, initially led by the illustrious Larry Barsness, who was touring Virginia City with his wife at a time when Charlie was trying to put together some entertainment for a miners' convention. The Barsnesses, intrigued by the problem, put together a skit called *Clem, the Miner's Daughter, or, Lord Help Us!* for the convention. The miners loved it, and the Barsnesses stayed on for many years. The Smith and Boyd Livery was quickly converted, in 1949, to the Opera House for the Virginia City Players, who have continued to provide melodrama of acclaim since that time.

Bozeman journalist Dick Pace (1923-1991) became ensnared by Virginia City's charm while writing a feature story on the new rush to the Gulch, in 1948. "When I got out of the car, I felt at home," he said, "as if I really belonged here."

He became a frequent visitor, then a part-time resident, and finally ended the "affair" thirty-five years later, when he and his wife Jackie moved to the community.

The "sun-birds" generally flee Virginia City before winter sets in, leaving behind a hardy, and usually hearty, small community. But, cabin fever has been known to work its sorcery during the long winter, and Pace recalled the days when he would return in the spring and "walk cautiously until I'd sorted out who was mad at whom and then I could relax."

Pace dug into the history of the region with gusto, researching and interviewing "old timers." In addition to writing for the local paper, *The Madisonian,* he published his book *Golden Gulch: The Story of Montana's Fabulous Alder Gulch* in 1962. He often entertained visiting groups with talks on regional history.

BUMMER DAN

by Dick Pace

There were some arriving who didn't want to do anything much. One Dan McFadden had been with that first bunch to follow the discoveries into the gulch. In his past he had been known as a pretty good worker; some of the men with whom he moved into Alder Gulch from Bannack had known him in Colorado. By this time, though, he had acquired a nickname that told his story. As a hardworking miner he was virtually unknown, but as "Bummer" Dan McFadden he gained fame.

Dan apparently did pretty well without working when he first came into the gulch. Bumming his meals, his drinks, and his sleeping quarters must have been fairly easy during the early days of the camp when everyone was excited about the new mines.

As the excitement wore off and the work settled down to the back-breaking job that mining always is after the cream is gone from the top, Dan's job became harder too. Having to work as hard as they did for what they were getting, the miners became more reluctant to provide Dan's wherewithal. Finally they rebelled. He was pestering some men on their claims in the gulch, according to the story, when one of them swore disgustedly and told him to go dig his own gold.

Whining a bit about all the good ground being taken, Dan got no sympathy. Giving him a pan, a shovel, and a pick, they sent him packing up the side of a hill near where they were working. Looking down Wallace Street today you can see the scar on the side of a hill where Dan finally stopped and unhappily stuck his pick into the ground.

The miners were not geologists. They didn't realize Alder Creek had not always looked as it did during the summer of 1863; at one time it was much deeper and much wider. The spot where Dan stopped had once been a gravel bar in the original creek.

As a result, Bummer Dan stuck his pick into what turned out to be one of the richest claims in the gulch. Just how rich is hard to tell. Miners were always either exaggerating the wealth of a claim or playing it down. Some say Dan cleared several million but that's doubtful. He did clear quite a stake, enough to sell out later and buy a stage ticket elsewhere.

He settled down and worked hard on his lucky find. By October he felt he had enough to move on. Maybe he was thinking of going back to the states to some former romance, or maybe just to live it up; no record exists explaining why he decided to sell out. There's ample record that he did so because it was about this time Lady Luck's smile began fading.

***

Bummer Dan must not have known how to court Lady Luck. By leaving earlier he might have made it; instead he chose to leave on the first Virginia City–Bannack stage to be robbed. His chances wouldn't have been any better had he waited. That robbery was the first in a calculated campaign of lawlessness that finally ended in vigilante action.

GARRY WUNDERWALD

Reflections on Collections

In 1927, Charlie Bovey had bought two old cars—a 1908 Anderson Motor buggy ($12.50) and a 1909 Cameron, air-cooled, four cylinder ($20). The two old cars "provided the germ that became an obsession"—collecting the remnants of the American west.

Charlie and Sue Bovey were consummate collectors. Sue particularly enjoyed vintage clothing and toys, while Charlie was enamored with old cars and stagecoaches; together they collected everything from thimbles to buildings. Many of the objects were not yet considered "antique," but they couldn't stand to see them discarded.

The first building of their collection was acquired in 1940 when they learned that the Sullivan Saddlery in Fort Benton was about to be torn down. They bought the entire stock of saddles, harnesses, and tools along with the building, which was dismantled and moved to Great Falls.

The Boveys' visit to Henry Ford's Greenfield Village in Detroit triggered the idea for the creation of Old Town at the North Montana State Fairgrounds in Great Falls. Within a year they had acquired, in addition to the saddlery, a barber shop, saloon, fire station, and general store—all with period contents and furnishings. A two-story residence from Nevada City joined the collection. Old Town drew admiring crowds to the fairgrounds for nearly twenty years.

The couple's only child, Ford, was born into this near-frenzy of collecting, traveling, and restoration. He too would come to appreciate the history, enjoy collecting, and love Alder Gulch, to the extent he considered it to be home.

In 1952, Montana State University awarded honorary Master of Arts degrees to Charlie and Sue for their work in stimulating interest in Montana history and tradition, as well as for their pioneering preservation efforts. Sue was the first woman to be so honored in Montana.

In 1960, the Fair Board in Great Falls was anticipating some expansion of the fair and there was pressure to move Old Town from the pavilion building on the fairgrounds.

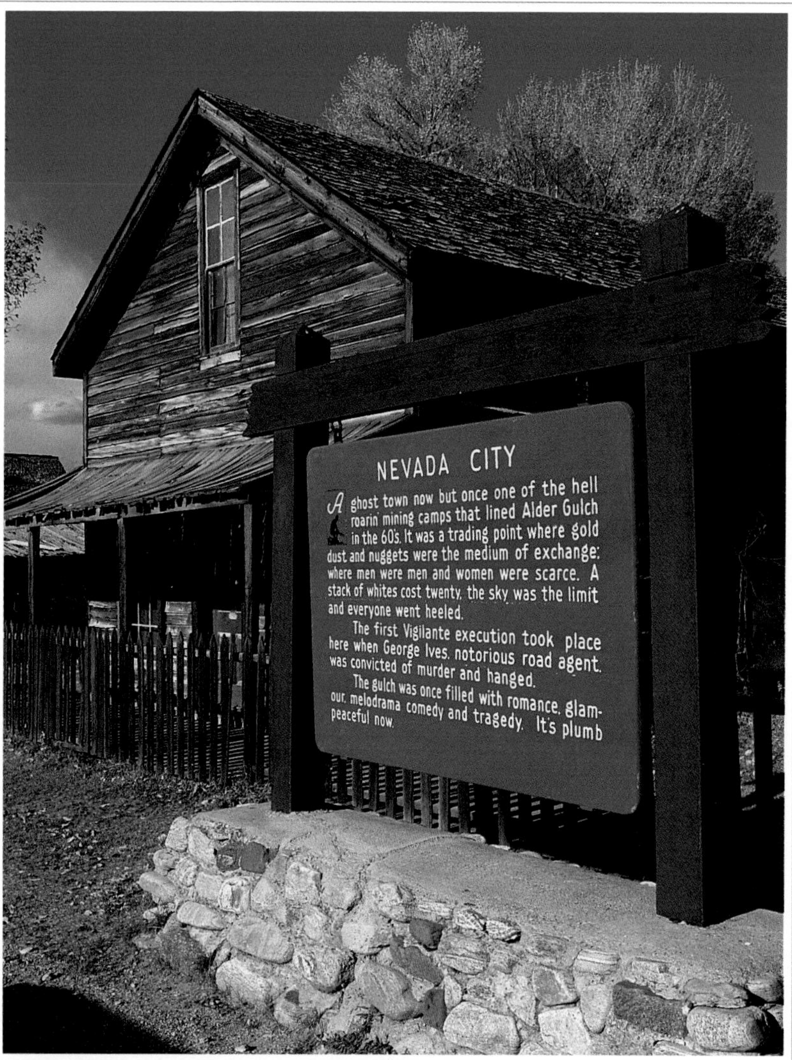

JOHN REDDY

GEORGE WUERTHNER

Above: *And Nevada City is plumb fun, too.*
Left: *A train's "chapel car" on exhibit in Nevada City.*

Facing page: *Mosey along, peaceful-like. Stop an' jaw a bit.*

Facing page: *Charles Bovey found Nevada City to be the perfect repository for many of his old buildings in need of new homes.*

Now Charlie Bovey had a second collection of buildings that needed a home. He began yet another development, this time at another of the "cities" along the gulch.

Nevada City, a scant two miles to the west of Virginia City, had also made a significant contribution to the history of Alder Gulch. It was part of the bustling "fourteen-mile city" complex of the early 1860s, with numerous businesses and a onetime population of several hundred. Noted as the scene of the trial and hanging of George Ives, Nevada City was also considered a stronghold of the Vigilantes. Dredging operations in the gulch, however, destroyed much of the visual evidence of the community.

Charlie purchased land, started saving what remained of the community and recreated the main street from building "parts" of a similar era, using a few surviving photos as a guide. He used Nevada City as a haven for buildings slated for demolition on their original sites. A firehall from Absaroka, the saddlery from Fort Benton, and parts of the Canyon Hotel from Yellowstone National Park found their way to the "new" community. The Stedman house, originally located in Nevada City, was returned after its stint at Old Town in Great Falls. The buildings also provided display space for an ever-growing collection, and additional facilities for guests.

There are many stories about the Senator from Great Falls who preferred to spend his leisure time in work clothes, rescuing old buildings from collapse. And what did he expect to get out of it? Frank Carey of Virginia City, responding to that question in 1948, said, "So far as I know, the money angle has never entered his head. He just likes to create. He spends his money here just as other wealthy men might spend it on race horses, or blooded cattle, or works of art, or airplanes or yachts. I think I know how he got into it, though. He was interested in history..."

In addition to love of history and collecting, Ford Bovey offered yet another observation about his parents when he said, "Living in the certainty of the past is far more comfortable than living in the uncertainty of the future."

When the profits from the the Bovey ranches were not enough to keep up with the work at "his cities," Charlie sold two of them. After the ranches were gone, his only comment was, "Well, thank heaven. At least I'm out of the purebred business." Charlie spent increasingly more time in southwestern Montana pursuing the work of Bovey Restorations, the company created to preserve and manage the properties in Virginia City and Nevada City.

Charlie readily admitted to being a "great starter, but a poor finisher," and he continued to start projects until his death in 1978. Sue continued to oversee the work, as president of Bovey Restorations, until her death ten years later. Their work in Virginia City is recognized as the first major privately funded preservation program in the nation.

Today, Ford fends off a multitude of problems to keep his parents' dream alive. Never profitable, the numerous buildings and collections are increasingly vulnerable to the ravages of time, weather, and ever-tightening economy. "Frankly," he says, "I'm running out of ranches to liquidate for support."

Bovey Restorations attempts to maintain over 110 buildings and contents in Virginia City and Nevada City, probably the largest collection of western Americana outside of the Smithsonian Institution. Although open for business only in the summer months, the buildings require year-round maintenance. Architects recently estimated the restoration costs for just two buildings in Virginia City at over $144,000.

A former mayor of Virginia City, Ford Bovey speaks to the burdens, responsibilities, and the profoundness of his legacy. With an insight fostered by growing up with the family's contribution, he said, "Dad knew best of all what an all-consuming job he had started—in some ways it is like he is getting even with me for some of the gray hairs that I caused him."

GEORGE WUERTHNER

GARRY WUNDERWALD

Left: *Hebgen Lake in the peace of winter.*
Below: *The Virginia City Players performed in Nevada City's Criterion Hall after the earthquake, but would not risk performing in Virginia City's stone Opera House.*

Earthquake

At midnight on August 17, 1959, a destructive earthquake rocked southwestern Montana. Its epicenter was near Hebgen Lake approximately forty miles south of Virginia City, close to the northwest corner of Yellowstone National Park.

The side of a mountain in the upper Madison River canyon was displaced. The ensuing landslide dammed the river, cost the lives of twenty-eight campers in the area, cracked the spillway of Hebgen Dam, and caused significant damage to roads and buildings in the area. Historical data did not indicate an earthquake of this intensity, and the magnitude of the earth movement was a surprise to seismologists. There was concern that Hebgen Dam would fail and imperil the residents of the valley below. Plans were made to evacuate the nearby town of Ennis and the surrounding area.

The quake had a dramatic impact on Virginia City. Some residents from Ennis sought refuge here as daylight revealed the damage upstream, many tourists left the area, and some residents reportedly walked the streets that night, fearful of entering the buildings. The cornice of the Masonic Temple was toppled and the south pediment of the courthouse fell into the courtroom. The bell tower of the schoolhouse later was removed as a precaution. The Virginia City Players did not risk performing in the stone Opera House, but the show did go on at Criterion Hall in Nevada City.

WAYNE SCHERR

JOHN REDDY

The respectable side of the Virginia City cemetery, away from Boot Hill.

WAYNE SCHERR

Designated a National Historic Landmark in 1961, Virginia City was officially recognized for its significant role in western expansion as well as for being an intact gold-era town.

Virginia City Today

A hill rises on the northern side of the townsite of Virginia City, with two cemeteries at its crest, overlooking the community in Daylight Gulch below. The city cemetery occupies a lofty perch above the northeast side of the city center. Boot Hill, final resting place for the infamous five road agents hanged by Vigilantes, is segregated from the city plots off to their west.

Dreams and aspirations also "rest in peace" on this hillside, marked only by native grasses and shrubs. One such aspiration is the townsite itself, laid out with geometric "city" precision, on a faded paper plat, with no regard to the natural landforms. Virginia never grew into her nearly 580 acres of rolling landscape. When miners began to answer the call of gold in other areas, Virginia City occupied only about a third of the townsite; and the city center today remains

Media Siege

Virginia City became the focus of national attention in 1985, as the scene of the trial of "Mountain Men" Don and Dan Nichols. Fifty-three-year-old Don Nichols and his nineteen-year-old son were accused of kidnapping Olympic athlete Kari Swenson on July 15, 1984, near the Big Sky subdivision in Gallatin Canyon. They were also accused of killing a volunteer rescuer, Alan Goldstein, the following day.

The Nicholses had rejected the habits of organized society in favor of the isolation of the mountains, and by 1984 they were year-around, nomadic residents of the primitive area. They subsisted on a network of "mountain gardens," improvised shelters, wild game, and caches of purchased supplies. They were seeking a woman for their family at the time they abducted Swenson, who was on a training run.

Swenson was seriously wounded during the initial volunteer rescue attempt on July 16 and was abandoned by the Nicholses as they fled from their encampment. Their get-away triggered a five-month manhunt that involved numerous law enforcement and federal officials, crossed county jurisdictions, and mobilized sophisticated technologies, local outdoorsmen, and additional volunteers. The ruggedness, complexity, and size of the Spanish Peaks Wilderness Area thwarted the efforts of the searchers throughout the summer and fall of 1984. Ironically, Madison County Sheriff Johnny France captured the pair on December 13, 1984, on the ranch where he grew up. France was portrayed as a modern-day hero in the saga, the *Great Falls Tribune* calling him the "lone lawman who wouldn't quit til he got his man." Neighboring Gallatin County Sheriff John Onstad and his deputies participated with Madison County throughout the manhunt and capture.

The trials began in the Madison County seat of Virginia City early in May of 1985. The Nicholses were tried separately.

From its commanding site, on the south side of the town's main street, the stately and monumental 1875 brick courthouse accommodated the two highly visible trials during the next three months. District Judge Frank Davis of Dillon issued strict guidelines to the press, one of which was a dress code stating that "reporters shall not be dressed in a manner to set them apart from other spectators." He would allow only one television camera in the courtroom. Montana Television Network, with four stations, was selected to run television production. They dedicated about $150,000 worth of equipment to the task, with a sophisticated control center located in a "shack" behind the courthouse. A CBS crew from Los Angeles, three Salt Lake City television stations, and two other Montana stations were on hand for what turned into a major media event. In addition, *The New York Times*, *Washington Post*, *Chicago Tribune*, *Denver Post*, and *Time* magazine correspondents were lined up only to hear Judge Davis instruct jurors, witnesses, and attorneys not to discuss the case with the media. In the words of *Madisonian* publisher, Daryl Tichenor, "There were so many reporters and so little going on that the reporters were interviewing each other."

Virginia City, which generally serves the needs of fewer than 200 people until after Memorial Day, scrambled to provide lodging and food for the host of witnesses, spectators, attorneys, and media.

Attorney Marc Racicot (elected Governor of Montana in 1992) was prosecutor for the trial, and Dan Nichols was ultimately sentenced to twenty years and six months in prison for kidnapping and assault. Don Nichols was found guilty of kidnapping and of the murder of Alan Goldstein; in July 1985 he was sentenced to 85 years of incarceration.

With press coverage tightly controlled, in and out of the courtroom, Virginia City "resources" starred in many news productions—putting the community "on the map."

A resident's response to that remark? "Hell, we've been on the map ever since there was a map."

A.B. SHELDON

Fish that Walk?

Virginia City saloon-keepers have been known in the past to remove an axolotl from an aquarium and give it a walk down the bar.

Equipped with both gills and lungs, the fish that walks isn't really a fish, but a form of salamander that doesn't fully develop into what the well-matured salamander should be. Madison County axolotl are the young of the terrestrial blotched tiger salamanders of the genus *Ambystoma tigrinum melanostictum.*

Well known in Mexico, and considered a delicacy, axolotl also occur in certain lakes of the Rocky Mountain region. Blue Lake in the Gravelly Mountains a few miles southeast of Virginia City contains Montana's only documented population of the curious amphibians. The lake is one of more than a dozen small glacial lakes or potholes known collectively as Axolotl Lakes.

Hatched from eggs, in the water, the young larval salamanders have bushy gills above and behind the jaws, a fin along the top of the tail, and four stubby legs. Normally, metamorphosis to a land-roving mature salamander takes a year or so, but for reasons unknown, the axolotl becomes sexually mature while still in the larval stage and does not lose the external gills and finned tail.

Originally regarded as a distinct species, the truth about the axolotl was accidentally discovered in Paris in 1865 when some of the strange creatures lost their gills and were transformed into perfect *Ambystomas*. Further experiments documented the metamorphosis, but it has not been explained why axolotl get stymied in their development. Habitat is believed to be the most likely cause.

Residents of the Social City historically enjoyed the recreational opportunities presented by the Axolotl Lakes area. By 1903, the Virginia City Axolotl Club had built a clubhouse near the largest body of water, Axolotl Lake. Boats were available for fishing for planted trout, which are efficient predators of larval or adult salamanders.

James A. Henshall and two friends trolling from a canvas boat in 1907 caught eleven trout with a combined weight of 70 pounds. The largest of the catch weighed thirteen pounds, considered to be an extraordinary weight for a five-year-old trout.

In 1976, the Axolotl Lakes Natural Area was established by the Bureau of Land Management to protect the habitat of the axolotl of Blue Lake. The approximately 1,520-acre area is open to hunting and fishing, but motor vehicles are prohibited.

A particularly notable axolotl, Oscar, resided in the V.C. Thompson–Hickman Museum for four years as the only live exhibit. When Oscar disappeared from the museum in August 1950, the *Madisonian* reported that it was under "circumstances indicating foul play." His disappearance shared headlines with the Korean War in newspapers around the state.

Along with their requests for his return, museum officials issued detailed instructions to the "fish-nappers" for the care and feeding of Oscar, who would not deign to eat if his food was not properly presented. The disappearance remains a mystery.

clustered in a small area, with only a few, scattered buildings beyond.

Streets named for the "discovery" team, vigilantes, politicians, and even presidents exist only on maps. In reality, only random roads on the steep terrain allow access to many areas within the townsite.

The dream of being the state capital lies there too, visually indistinguishable in the landscape from the imaginary streets. More than three acres, set aside and held for 125 years, have only the words "Capitol Square" on a map as evidence of their intended use.

The current community wouldn't have it any other way. Fiercely protective of both the surrounding landscape and Virginia City's colorful history, the residents also are protective of their quality of life. Had the Montana Supreme Court of 1874 ruled in favor of Virginia City retaining the Territorial Capital title, the quality of life as they know it would be "history."

Imagine modern state government buildings on the Virginia City townsite! The landscape that residents cherish would be gone, along with the lifestyle that continues to attract people to the community, both to visit and to live. Naturally the history of this special place can never be erased, but the visual evidence remains vulnerable to change.

Virginia City today commands considerable attention because of its amazing resemblance to the Virginia City of the 1860s. Political affairs, mining, and social activities so important to the history of the community continue to be the mainstays of the economy. Small-scale gold mining continues in Alder Gulch, and some residents also work at the Cypress Hills Talc mines near Ennis.

The business of Madison County is still conducted in Virginia City. The county spreads over an area of 3,586.5 square miles, with a population of slightly less than 6,000. The large rural county contains a high percentage of federal land, which provides little economic strength in terms of taxable valuation. Perched midway between the Madison and Jefferson valleys, centrally located Virginia City remains a good place for the seat of Madison County government. The county reciprocates by pro-

JOHN REDDY

Country-style accommodations.

viding year-round jobs and activities that contribute to the local economy.

Virginia City, the fourth-largest community in the county, operated on an annual budget comparable to that of one average American family until a highly controversial three-percent resort tax started adding to the city's coffers in 1991. According to the 1990 census, of the 140 people who call Virginia City home, 112 are adult (over age 18). There are 66 households. The population count increases dramatically during the summer, and likewise drops during the winter. Many who own homes in Virginia City spend only summers or holidays in the community, along with a transient summer population, which comes to provide a work force for the seasonal restaurants, hotels, shops and theater.

The limited economy, occasionally harsh climate, isolation, and lack of amenities have spawned residents of fundamental self-reliance, considerable realism, and earthy good humor. Small enough to make decisions by democratic consensus, the community fosters strong opinions and open discussions. The Pioneer Bar, Virginia City Cafe, and Rank's general store—the only year-round businesses—are likely to be the "scenes of political unrest" on any given day. It is difficult to remain aloof from community affairs in Virginia City. The town is not large enough, and there is too much to do. Interaction is generally expected. Almost everyone will serve, in some capacity, in the government of the community—on boards, committees, councils, or even as mayor. Medical emergencies are handled by the volunteer Quick Response Unit, and the fire department is also made up of volunteers.

The city wrestles with fundamental issues such as water, sewer, and fire services, esoteric issues such as protective zoning and ordinances for its historic buildings, and issues of detail such as whether the city clerk's dog can attend council meetings. The spirit of the place has been unquenchable since 1863, through adversity and good fortune.

"Virginia City is a tar-baby," says Tim Gor-

DENNIS J. CWIDAK

One Virginia City resident was quick to point out, "We know we don't live in the real world."

don, who summers in the community and operates the Montana Picture Gallery, where patrons can pose in costumes of the 1860s for photographs. The majority of the residents seem to fall into two categories—those who are multi-generation, descendants of pioneers, or those who stepped in the "tar" and got stuck here.

Bob Gabler arrived in Virginia City for summer employment with Bovey Restorations nineteen years ago, and explains that he's still there because of an "accidental love affair" with the community. Now doing business as Alder Gulch Outfitters, Bob offers summer rafting excursions on the Jefferson, Madison, and Big Hole rivers, and will soon have his own line of Made-in-Montana outdoor wear.

From the time John Ellingsen was eight years old, he looked forward to annual vacations with his mother, which always included a stay in Virginia City. Years later, armed with degrees in industrial arts and history, John was ready and eager to return. John's intense interest in preserving the resources of Virginia and Nevada cities landed him a job with Charlie Bovey in 1972. As of 1993, Ellingsen was still the curator of Bovey Restorations.

Perhaps it is that "light, dry air, which results in an expansive feeling and a heartier and more cordial spirit"; or the history which seems to permeate everyone and everything; or the hunting and fishing in the area; or the feeling of family, real or implied; or the "comfort of living in the certainty of the past," as Ford Bovey put it. People are drawn to Virginia City, and some are pretty resourceful in devising ways to stay there.

"Everyone in Montana is in love with this little place," remarked U.S. Representative Pat Williams of Montana. "It represents a cradle of Montana history."

Virginia City residents wholeheartedly agree with that conclusion, but it doesn't create many jobs; and the jobs that are created usually last only through the summer months. Local government, mining, retail trade, and construction provide the majority of year-round employment in the community, with ten or fewer employed in each category. According to the 1990 census, fewer than five were employed in manufacturing or business and repair services. Three enterprising women commute about twenty miles from their Sheridan homes to open the doors of the restaurant and general store, and they cheerfully serve the small winter population.

Numerous shops open for the tourist season, but they generally offer merchandise geared for the tourist crowd and not the staples required for everyday living. The crush of summer tourism also strains the community's limited water, sewer, and garbage systems, which are basically designed for a small year-round occupancy. Although residents enjoy the excitement and activity of the summer, for the most part, they are just as happy when the season is over. "It's like living in a fishbowl," according to one resident. "People come up and look in your windows."

Virginia City may look like an 1860s ghost town, but as satellite dishes in many yards testify, it is a community of the 1990s. One in the community, however, was quick to point out, "We know we don't live in the real world."

The satellite dishes also speak of the remoteness of the area. There is no television cable service to the community, and the surrounding terrain discourages even radio transmission. "Remoteness makes us what we are," offered one resident, and perhaps it adds to the sense of community. Travel out of the community is required for most needs, even gasoline. Unlike city dwellers, residents go to the post office for their mail, and they even haul their own garbage.

Virginia Citians are not overwhelmingly in agreement about growth in the community,

GARRY WUNDERWALD

Maybe the drive-through is open. And I have my cash card if I can find the machine.

but the majority would like to see just enough of a population increase to support a few more basic services. The community is subjected to new and increased pressures as southwest Montana experiences "growing pains." Madison was one of few Montana counties to increase in population in the last decade. Recently discovered for its quality of life and recreational opportunity, Virginia City has seen significant impact in adjacent valleys—summer homes and ranchettes now dot the landscape. Retirees, recreationists, "glitterati," and escapists from urban congestion are discovering the area, but again, generate seasonal services and strain the existing infrastructure of the county.

Virginia City is alluring, nestled in the middle of this growth area in an isolation created by historical circumstances and rugged terrain. She offers a rare opportunity to step back through the years into the very creation of Montana. Unlike many mining camps of territorial days, she still supports a community that has continued to preserve and protect the visual evidence of that history.

TIME LINE

1803 Louisiana Purchase
1804-1806 Lewis and Clark Expedition
1841 St. Mary's mission established in the Bitterroot Valley
1843-1846 Fort Benton (originally called Fort Lewis) established
1846 Oregon Territory created
1849 Gold rush to California
1851 Fort Laramie Treaty and 1855 Isaac Stevens negotiations stipulate that southwest Montana is common hunting ground for all Indian peoples
1856 Buildings in Montana:
Cantonment Stevens, church at St. Ignatius
Fort Owen
Fort Benton
Fort Union
structures at Jocko River
1858-1859 Gold in Colorado—Pike's Peak
1859 May, Comstock Lode discovered at Virginia City, Nevada
1859 Washington Territory created
1860 Mullan road completed to Fort Benton
1861 April 12, Civil War begins with shelling of Fort Sumter
1862 July 28, Gold discovered at Bannack
1863 Idaho Territory created

1863

Alder Gulch

May 26, Fairweather party finds gold at Alder Gulch—Tom Cover, Henry Edgar, Bill Fairweather, Barney Hughes, Harry Rodgers, Michael Sweeney
June 6, Fairweather Mining District organized
July, second log cabin in Ruby Valley built by Jean Baptiste Laurin
July, Summit Mining District organized
December, Nicholas Tiebalt killed by Innocents
December 21, George Ives hanged in Nevada City

Virginia City

June 16, Varina Town Co. records 320-acre site in Idaho Territory
Mechanical Bakery—first permanent commercial building
A.J. Oliver establishes the first stage service
Lower floor of Rank's Drugstore built
A. Toponce builds first sluice in Gulch
Kiskadden barn constructed
July, pony express established to Fort Bridger
December 23, Vigilante organizational meeting

1864

January 10, Plummer hanged at Bannack
March 10, Jack Slade hanged by Vigilantes
May 26, Montana Territory created from Idaho Territory
June 22, President Lincoln appoints Sidney Edgerton governor of Montana Territory; Territorial seal (today the state seal) designed
July 14, Gold discovered at Last Chance Gulch

Alder Gulch

Union City established at Oro Cache lode; its main street named Lincoln Boulevard
January, first quartz lode mine, at Summit
Virginia City and Summit wagon road chartered by first legislature—winter 1864-65

Virginia City

January 14, five road agents hanged at "Hangman's" building in Virginia City
July, both Jim Bridger and John Bozeman bring wagon trains to Virginia City
Dimsdale appointed Superintendent of Public Instruction for Montana Territory
August, first school opens, in temporary church on Idaho Street
August 27, *Montana Post* first issue, 960 copies at 50¢ each
Area population: 7,000—spring; 18,000—autumn (by some estimates)
Flour famine—winter of 1864-65

1865

March 9, Civil War ends
March 14, President Lincoln assassinated
August 4, President Johnson appoints Thomas Meagher secretary of Montana Territory

Alder Gulch

Junction City laid out—population 100 in 1872

Virginia City

Baptist church dedicated
Montana Historical Society forms; meets at Dance & Stuart's store
January 2, Con Orem vs. Hugh O'Neil prizefight at Leviathon Hall—185 rounds in 3 hours, 5 minutes
December 25, Catholic church dedicated in a converted theater (razed 1930); Mass by Father Giorda

1866

Virginia City

November 2, Telegraph service established to Salt Lake City

1867

July 1, Thomas Meagher dies in Fort Benton

Virginia City

March 17, St. Paul's Episcopal parish organized; original Episcopal church built
December 27, Masonic temple dedicated

1868

Alder Gulch

Seven-stamp mill built at Summit
Nevada City begins to decline

Virginia City

January 18, Skating pond in Virginia City inaugurated
March 14, Leviathon Hall razed
March, *Montana Post* moves to Helena

1869

May 11, transcontinental railroad completed

1872

March 1, Yellowstone National Park established by act of Congress

Alder Gulch

Adobetown population: 150

1873
Madisonian begins publication

1875
Territorial capital moves to Helena
Virginia City
Courthouse completed
Grace Methodist church built

1876
Virginia City brick school built

1879
Alder Gulch
Adobetown population: 425—175 Caucasian, 250 Chinese

1889
November 8, Montana becomes a state

1892
Virginia City
Electricity arrives

1896-97
Alder Gulch
First dredge

1897
Virginia City
City Hall (Elks club) built

1897-98
Alder Gulch
Dredge *Maggie Gibson* brought from Bannack

1901
Alder Gulch
Northern Pacific Railroad builds branch line to Alder
Town of Ruby built for dredge company employees—estimated population of 500

1902
Alder Gulch
Two electric stacker dredges built at Ruby
Virginia City
St. Paul's Episcopal church built of stone

1903
Alder Gulch
Resurgence of mining at Summit—new 60-stamp Kearsarge mill
November 6, Mining disaster at Kearsarge; eight lives lost

1906
Alder Gulch
Electricity furnished to Ruby by Madison Electric Co.

1910
Alder Gulch
Largest electric dredge in world built at Ruby

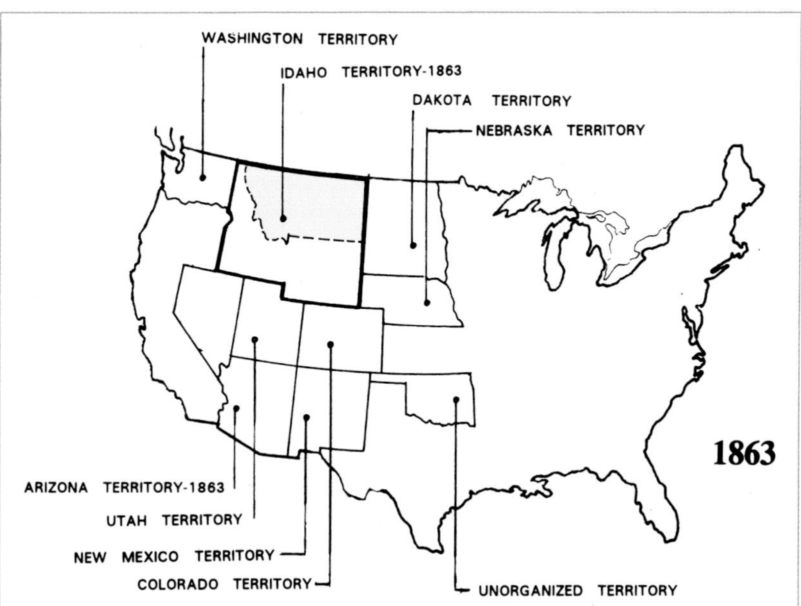

1917
U.S. enters World War I

1922
Alder Gulch
Dredge operation ceases in Gulch

1930s
Alder Gulch
Humphrey's dry gold dredges work in Gulch

1942
Government mandates no gold mining during World War II (nonessential industry)

1940s
Virginia City
Bovey family begins work in Virginia City

1948
Highway 287 to Virginia City paved

1959
August 17, Madison earthquake; 28 lives lost

1960-61
Alder Gulch
Boveys begin work in Nevada City

1972
Virginia City
July 1, fire at Madison County Courthouse

1973
Virginia City
Autumn, groundbreaking for new courthouse

1983
Virginia City
May 13, fire at Bale-of-Hay saloon; Mechanical Bakery damaged

WAYNE SCHERR

FOR FURTHER READING

Alt, David D., and Donald W. Hyndman. *Roadside Geology of the Northern Rockies.* Missoula: Mountain Press Publishing Co., 1972.

Barsness, Larry. *Gold Camp.* New York: Hastings House, 1962.

Bertsche, William H. Jr., and Helen Fitzgerald Sanders. *X. Beidler Vigilante* Norman: University of Oklahoma Press, 1957.

Brier, Warren J. *The Frightful Punishment.* Missoula: University of Montana Press, 1969.

Callaway, Lew L. *Montana's Righteous Hangmen.* Norman: University of Oklahoma Press, 1982.

Dimsdale, Thomas J. *The Vigilantes of Montana.* Butte: McKee Printing Co., 1950.

France, John, and Malcolm McConnell. *Incident at Big Sky.* New York: W.W. Norton & Co.,1986.

Graves, F. Lee. *Bannack: Cradle of Montana.* Helena: American & World Geographic Publishing, 1991.

Herndon, Sarah Raymond. *Days on the Road: Crossing the Plains in 1865.* N.Y.: Burr Printing House, 1902.

Howard, Joseph Kinsey. *Montana High, Wide and Handsome.* New Haven: Yale University Press, 1959.

Johnson, Dorothy. *The Bloody Bozeman.* N. Y.: McGraw Hill Book Co.,1971.

Langford, Nathaniel. *Vigilante Days and Ways.* Missoula: University of Montana Press, 1957.

Madison County History Association. *Pioneer Trails And Trials.* 1976.

Malone, Michael P., and Richard B. Roeder. *Montana, A History of Two Centuries.* Seattle: University of Washington Press, 1976.

Pace, Dick. *Golden Gulch: The Story of Montana's Fabulous Alder Gulch.* 2nd ed. Virginia City: Virginia City Trading Company, 1970.

Ronan, Margaret. "Memoirs of a Frontier Woman: Mary C. Ronan." Unpublished master's thesis, Montana State University, 1932. Published as: *Frontier Woman: The Story of Mary Ronan as Told to Margaret Ronan*; Edited by H.G. Merriam. Missoula: University of Montana, 1973.

Spence, Clark C. *Territorial Politics and Government in Montana 1864–89.* Urbana: University of Illinois Press, 1975.

Stout, Tom. *Montana: Its Story and Biography,* Vol. 1. Chicago: The American Historical Society, 1921.

Stuart, Granville. *Pioneering in Montana: The Making of a State , 1864–87.* Lincoln: University of Nebraska Press, 1925.

Toponce, Alexander. *Reminiscences of Alexander Toponce.* Norman: University of Oklahoma Press, 1971.

Wolle, Muriel Sibell. *Montana Pay Dirt.* Chicago: The Swallow Press Inc., 1963.

INDEX

William Boyce Thompson built the Thompson–Hickman Museum in 1918 as a memorial to his father and his father-in-law. The donated museum is maintained by the Vigilance Club of Virginia City. A library is housed on the top floor.

WAYNE SCHERR

All About Montana...All Year Long **_Montana Magazine_**

The insider's guide to enjoying Montana ... in sumptuous color photography and fun-to-read features.

Every issue explores the colorful, the quixotic, the uniquely Montana lifestyle, and features wild critters and colorful characters.

- hunting and fishing • history • personalities
- wild country
- humor
- Montana book reviews

...and always a center section of Montana wildlife and scenic color photography.

Six times a year. $18. Credit cards accepted. In Montana call 1-800-821-3874, outside Montana call 1-800-654-1105.

Montana Geographic Series

For an in-depth perspective about the places that make Montana special there is no better source than the Montana Geographic Series. For almost a decade the Montana Geographic Series has explored rivers, mountains, wildlife and wildlands in 19 titles. Each features more than 100 pages with 35,000 to 50,000 words of text by an acknowledged expert, and each is illustrated with more than 100 color photos. You'll recognize the unique horizontal format (11" x $8^1/_2$") and the colorful covers that make a set of "geographics" a household treasure.